OPPOSING VIEWPOINTS® SERIES

Eco-Architecture

Other Books of Related Interest:

Opposing Viewpoints Series

Coal

Doomsday Scenarios

Garbage and Recycling

Urban Agriculture

At Issue Series

Are Mass Extinctions Inevitable?

Should There Be an International Climate Treaty?

The US Energy Grid

What Is the Impact of E-Waste?

Current Controversies Series

Pollution

Introducing Issues with Opposing Viewpoints

Endangered Species

Energy Alternatives

Environmentalism

Global Warming

Issues That Concern You

Nuclear Power

"Congress shall make no law . . . abridging the freedom of speech, or of the press."

First Amendment to the US Constitution

The basic foundation of our democracy is the First Amendment guarantee of freedom of expression. The Opposing Viewpoints series is dedicated to the concept of this basic freedom and the idea that it is more important to practice it than to enshrine it.

OPPOSING VIEWPOINTS® SERIES

Eco-Architecture

Roman Espejo, Book Editor

GREENHAVEN PRESS
A part of Gale, Cengage Learning

GALE
CENGAGE Learning·

Detroit • New York • San Francisco • New Haven, Conn • Waterville, Maine • London

GALE
CENGAGE Learning·

Elizabeth Des Chenes, *Director, Publishing Solutions*

© 2013 Greenhaven Press, a part of Gale, Cengage Learning.

Gale and Greenhaven Press are registered trademarks used herein under license.

For more information, contact:
Greenhaven Press
27500 Drake Rd.
Farmington Hills, MI 48331-3535
Or you can visit our Internet site at gale.cengage.com

For product information and technology assistance, contact us at

Gale Customer Support, 1-800-877-4253
For permission to use material from this text or product, submit all requests online at
www.cengage.com/permissions

Further permissions questions can be emailed to permissionrequest@cengage.com

Articles in Greenhaven Press anthologies are often edited for length to meet page requirements. In addition, original titles of these works are changed to clearly present the main thesis and to explicitly indicate the author's opinion. Every effort is made to ensure that Greenhaven Press accurately reflects the original intent of the authors. Every effort has been made to trace the owners of copyrighted material.

Cover Image copyright © Marcin-linfernum/Shutterstock.com.

LIBRARY OF CONGRESS CATALOGING-IN-PUBLICATION DATA

Eco-architecture / Roman Espejo, book editor.
    p. cm. -- (Opposing viewpoints)
  Includes bibliographical references and index.
    ISBN 978-0-7377-6320-1 (hardcover) -- ISBN 978-0-7377-6321-8 (pbk.)
  1. Sustainable architecture. 2. Sustainable buildings. I. Espejo, Roman, 1977- editor of compilation.
    NA2542.36.E264 2012
    720'.47--dc23
                                                    2012006924

Printed in the United States of America
1 2 3 4 5   16 15 14 13 12

FD254

Contents

Chapter 3: How Is Eco-Architecture Being Implemented?

Chapter 4: How Can Eco-Architecture Be Encouraged in the Future?

Why Consider Opposing Viewpoints?

> "The only way in which a human being can make some approach to knowing the whole of a subject is by hearing what can be said about it by persons of every variety of opinion and studying all modes in which it can be looked at by every character of mind. No wise man ever acquired his wisdom in any mode but this."
>
> John Stuart Mill

In our media-intensive culture it is not difficult to find differing opinions. Thousands of newspapers and magazines and dozens of radio and television talk shows resound with differing points of view. The difficulty lies in deciding which opinion to agree with and which "experts" seem the most credible. The more inundated we become with differing opinions and claims, the more essential it is to hone critical reading and thinking skills to evaluate these ideas. Opposing Viewpoints books address this problem directly by presenting stimulating debates that can be used to enhance and teach these skills. The varied opinions contained in each book examine many different aspects of a single issue. While examining these conveniently edited opposing views, readers can develop critical thinking skills such as the ability to compare and contrast authors' credibility, facts, argumentation styles, use of persuasive techniques, and other stylistic tools. In short, the Opposing Viewpoints Series is an ideal way to attain the higher-level thinking and reading skills so essential in a culture of diverse and contradictory opinions.

In addition to providing a tool for critical thinking, Opposing Viewpoints books challenge readers to question their own strongly held opinions and assumptions. Most people form their opinions on the basis of upbringing, peer pressure, and personal, cultural, or professional bias. By reading carefully balanced opposing views, readers must directly confront new ideas as well as the opinions of those with whom they disagree. This is not to argue simplistically that everyone who reads opposing views will—or should—change his or her opinion. Instead, the series enhances readers' understanding of their own views by encouraging confrontation with opposing ideas. Careful examination of others' views can lead to the readers' understanding of the logical inconsistencies in their own opinions, perspective on why they hold an opinion, and the consideration of the possibility that their opinion requires further evaluation.

Evaluating Other Opinions

To ensure that this type of examination occurs, Opposing Viewpoints books present all types of opinions. Prominent spokespeople on different sides of each issue as well as well-known professionals from many disciplines challenge the reader. An additional goal of the series is to provide a forum for other, less known, or even unpopular viewpoints. The opinion of an ordinary person who has had to make the decision to cut off life support from a terminally ill relative, for example, may be just as valuable and provide just as much insight as a medical ethicist's professional opinion. The editors have two additional purposes in including these less known views. One, the editors encourage readers to respect others' opinions—even when not enhanced by professional credibility. It is only by reading or listening to and objectively evaluating others' ideas that one can determine whether they are worthy of consideration. Two, the inclusion of such viewpoints encourages the important critical thinking skill of objectively evaluating an author's credentials and bias. This evaluation will illuminate an author's reasons for taking a particular stance on an issue and will aid in readers' evaluation of the author's ideas.

It is our hope that these books will give readers a deeper understanding of the issues debated and an appreciation of the complexity of even seemingly simple issues when good and honest people disagree. This awareness is particularly important in a democratic society such as ours in which people enter into public debate to determine the common good. Those with whom one disagrees should not be regarded as enemies but rather as people whose views deserve careful examination and may shed light on one's own.

Thomas Jefferson once said that "difference of opinion leads to inquiry, and inquiry to truth." Jefferson, a broadly educated man, argued that "if a nation expects to be ignorant and free . . . it expects what never was and never will be." As individuals and as a nation, it is imperative that we consider the opinions of others and examine them with skill and discernment. The Opposing Viewpoints series is intended to help readers achieve this goal.

David L. Bender and Bruno Leone,
Founders

Introduction

"There is a lot of hype about prefabri-cated architecture. It has become the 'Holy Grail' that students want to learn, and the environmentally sustainable methodology that many clients want to build."

—Fredrick H. Zal and
Kendra Cox, "Pre.Fab:
Myth, Hype + Reality,"
Without a Hitch—New Directions
in Prefabricated Architecture

About 2 to 3 percent of homes in the United States are modular, according to the National Association of Home Builders. A modular home is delivered by trucks to the site in prefabricated sections and placed on the foundation by a crane. Typically, manufacturing can take several weeks or months, and on-site assembly can be completed in a few hours or days. "The modular factory system combines engineering know-how and factory-production methods to design and build more efficiently and with greater quality control," claims Andrew Gianino is his book *The Modular Home.*

Prefabricated homes have been available in the United States since the 1890s. Delivered via railroad, they were purchased through mail-order catalogs; a "mail-order home" kit from Sears contained thirty thousand pieces—including 750 pounds of nails and twenty-seven gallons of paint—and came with a seventy-five-page instruction manual for homeowners. In its first "Modern Homes" catalog, Sears offered forty-four designs, with prices ranging from $695 to $4,199. The relative popularity of prefab housing waned during the Great Depression, but rebounded after World War II, when returning soldiers increased the demand for affordable homes. In the following decades, however, the preference for traditionally constructed houses would prevail. "Today, there is still a bit of a romantic notion that building custom home floor plans on site piece-by-piece is somehow superior. This belief lingers even though consumers would reject new appliances and automobiles that were built in someone's backyard, with the materials exposed to the weather and with no one watching over the assembly," Gianino maintains.

A new generation of builders aims to change the image of modular homes and reduce the environmental impacts of housing. Because it departs from the building of stick-built homes, prefab housing has emerged at the forefront of eco-architecture. "The modular housing industry likes to say that it has always had a few characteristics that today might be considered eco-friendly—from reduced waste to a smaller construction footprint," says Nick Chambers, a green journalist, in the *New York Times*. For example, he maintains that modular homes are built with thicker walls and floors and joined with screws and glue—rather than nails—to hold up during transport over long distances. "A side effect of this, industry representatives note: Higher energy efficiency due to the extra insulation and tighter, less draft-prone seams," asserts Chambers. Also, modular-home builders tout factory fabrication as being greener than on-site building by generating less waste with its assembly and construction practices. "Building modules are shipped to the site up to 95 percent completed, resulting in fewer construction pollutants and better protection of green space and habitat," asserts NRB, a company that specializes in modular building. "There are fewer material deliveries and workforce travel requirements to the project site, which means [greenhouse gas] emissions are reduced," adds NRB.

In 2009 Clayton Homes, one of the largest manufacturers of prefab houses and mobile homes in the nation, launched i-house, its ambitious line of luxury modular homes. It is available in two floor plans that can be configured in several ways: a one-bedroom, one-bath at 723 square feet and a one-bedroom, two-bath with a detached flex room at 991 square feet. Features such as a butterfly roof for collecting rainwater, renewable bamboo flooring, and paints free of volatile organic compounds (VOCs) come standard with the i-house. Options include solar panels that halve the home's electricity consumption, tankless water heaters, and low-flow faucets. Depending on the floor plan, configuration, and state, prices start from around $80,000 or $100,000. "Manufactured housing is a highly regulated industry, with three distinct qualities: manufactured homes are safe, they are energy efficient, and they are affordable," declares Kevin Clayton, president and chief executive officer. In 2010 the manufacturer unveiled i-house 2.0, a concept for a new floor plan with additional bedrooms.

Numerous commentators, nonetheless, propose that modular homes have their shortcomings. In a student research project by Oklahoma State University, investigators argue that most are not eco-friendly by design. "Because manufactured homes should be portable, lightweight, and designed before site selection, they are not climate-specific, not site-responsive, and lose the benefit of thermal mass," they contend. "That is why manufactured homes are not energy efficient, i.e., unsustainable." Modular Today, an independent reviewer of the industry, asserts that fortifying prefab housing against the stresses of shipment consumes significant resources. "So the material saved by creating less waste is equalized by the extra material needed for transporting," it observes. And some consumers complain that even high-end modular homes have not overcome their reputation for lacking curb appeal. "Their interior is every bit as attractive as some of the expensive homes, but the outside still reminds me of the temporary restrooms in an urban highway rest stop," quips an online commentator about the i-house on FastCompany.com. "We are in the 21st century, why the continued reliance on the cold and foreboding '50s modern idioms?"

Modular homes attempt to address the concerns of green building: home size, construction waste, pollution, energy efficiency, and conservation of resources and the environment. In *Opposing Viewpoints: Eco-Architecture*, these issues and more are explored in the following chapters: Is Eco-Architecture Beneficial?, How Does Eco-Architecture Impact the Environment?, How Is Eco-Architecture Being Implemented?, and How Can Eco-Architecture Be Encouraged in the Future? The diverse and impassioned arguments selected for this volume demonstrate how the built environment is the foundation for a cleaner future.

OPPOSING
VIEWPOINTS®
SERIES

CHAPTER 1

Is Eco-Architecture Beneficial?

Chapter Preface

Passive solar design is one of the essentials of green building, in which windows, walls, and floors maximize solar heat during the winter and minimize it in the summer. "Unlike active solar heating systems, passive solar design doesn't involve the use of mechanical and electrical devices, such as pumps, fans, or electrical controls to move the solar heat," states the US Department of Energy (DOE). "Passive solar homes range from those heated almost entirely by the sun to those with south-facing windows that provide some fraction of the heating load," the DOE adds.

Five elements are needed for passive solar design to be complete for a building or home, according to the DOE. The aperture, or collector, is a window. Ideally, it faces true south within 30 degrees and is not shaded by buildings or trees in the morning and afternoon. The absorber is the dark, hard surface that collects solar heat, positioned to hit direct sunlight. The thermal mass is the material behind or under the surface of the absorber that stores solar heat. Distribution is the way the solar heat is circulated throughout the building or home; in true passive design, the natural methods of conduction, convection, and radiation are employed. Control includes roofs that prevent solar heat from entering the aperture during the summer as well as thermostats, vents, dampers, and other devices that limit or permit the flow of heat.

Some experts advise that a careful approach must be taken to passive solar design, however. For example, Martin Holladay, senior editor of GreenBuildingAdvisor.com, says that south-facing windows may have mixed results. "While it admits plenty of heat—sometimes too much heat—on sunny days, it can lose a lot of heat on cold nights," he claims. Holladay also insists that the structure must be adequately airtight and insulated, a mistake seen with the "solar houses" of the

1970s and 1980s. In the following chapter, the authors discuss the basics of eco-architecture and debate their potential benefits and pitfalls.

> "Greenness is generally a question of two issues—energy efficiency and the eco-friendliness of a building's materials—along with a broader sense of how a new house or apartment building ties into its local, regional, and global context."

Eco-Architecture Has Many Benefits

Alanna Stang and Christopher Hawthorne

Alanna Stang is editor in chief of Whole Living, *a sustainable living magazine. Christopher Hawthorne is the architecture critic for the* Los Angeles Times. *Stang and Hawthorne co-wrote* The Green House: New Directions in Sustainable Architecture. *In the following viewpoint, excerpted from* The Green House, *the authors discuss the principles of eco-architecture. At a basic level, according to the authors, a truly green building is constructed as small as possible and with every sustainable resource available; maximizes solar energy and shade and minimizes ecological damage; and is located near public transportation, workplaces, and schools. Additionally, architects and designers committed to sustainability, Stang and Hawthorne maintain, use energy-efficient technologies and designs, renewable resources, and strategies to create adaptable or architecturally valuable buildings with long, useful lives.*

As you read, consider the following questions:

1. In Stang and Hawthorne's view, what do most experts agree is the key to eco-architecture?

2. In the authors' opinion, what is most important about the origins of sustainable residential design?

3. To what did green architects pay most attention during the 1980s and 1990s, as claimed by the authors?

So what does it mean, exactly, to say that a house is "green"? It is difficult to define the term with complete precision. For starters, we like the straightforward suggestion from the David and Lucile Packard Foundation that "any building that has significantly lower negative environmental impacts than traditional buildings" qualifies as green. More broadly, the key, most experts agree, is a flexible and holistic approach that involves making careful, ecologically conscious decisions at every point in the planning, design, and construction processes while keeping in mind that the ideal solution may not always be evident. An architect or would-be homeowner deciding, for instance, between a kind of roofing material created in an environmentally wasteful manner but available locally and an eco-friendly variety that has to be trucked in from 2,500 miles away will not be helped much by a universal green design checklist. In general, though, there are steady guidelines to be followed and priorities to be kept in mind. Residential designs that aim for authentic greenness should, at the very least, be:

• as small as possible, for a house that uses every sustainable technique under the sun will not be as kind to the earth as practically any house half its size;

- positioned to take advantage of winter sun and summer shade, and to minimize damage to the plants, animals, soil, etc., already there;

- located as close to public transportation, workplaces, schools, and/or shopping as realistically possible.

Those are the basics; importantly, none of them need add any cost to the construction of a new home (save for the potentially higher prices of land in or near a city). Indeed, following the first rule will necessarily lead to lower building costs.

Beyond that, greenness is generally a question of two issues—energy efficiency and the eco-friendliness of a building's materials—along with a broader sense of how a new house or apartment building ties into its local, regional, and global context. Often, these concerns are intertwined, but in general architects committed to sustainability will employ many (and in rare cases all) of the following:

- recycled materials and even existing foundations or building shells;

- wood from stocks that are sustainably managed;

- materials that are low in embodied energy—that is, the energy required to extract and produce them as well as to deliver them to a building site;

- natural materials, such as bamboo, that can be easily replenished;

- efficient lighting systems that take advantage of daylight to reduce electricity needs or include sensors and timers that shut off lights when they are not in use;

- water systems that collect rainwater or treat so-called gray water (from sinks and showers) so that it can be reused for gardens or toilets;

- strategies to ensure that a house will have a long life because it is comfortable to spend time in, architecturally significant, or adaptable to future uses;

- insulation, glass, and facades that are energy efficient and that promote cooling by natural ventilation instead of by air-conditioning;

- features that take advantage of the sun's rays, either passively, using thermal massing and high-efficiency glass, or actively through photovoltaic panels, to turn sunlight into electricity;

- interior materials and finishes, from carpets to paints, that minimize chemical emissions and promote good air quality. . . .

True sustainability, of course, means a house that produces as much energy as it consumes. More than a few of the houses here would fail to qualify as green by that standard. For architects and clients alike, it is not always realistic to expect perfection. The point is to make careful, informed choices from selecting a site to picking out the cabinetry. Along with the idea that green houses are now being produced by many of the world's most talented architects, what we are interested in communicating here is the notion that sustainability is not exotic or better left to specialists, but based in the kind of common sense that is comprehensible for any potential home builder—or home buyer, for that matter.

It is true that building a new house of any kind will rarely be a positive environmental gesture. But no matter how ecologically progressive our society becomes, demand for new housing is not going to dry up any time soon. About 1.5 million single-family homes went up in the United States in 2003 alone, according to the National Association of Home Builders—the vast majority of them, sadly, following not a single green design principle. But more and more, architects are finding ways to reduce the margin between the amount of resources consumed in the construction and operation of a house and those saved or replenished. Indeed, by combining ancient techniques with the latest in super-efficient mechanical systems and materials, the designers ... are managing to make that margin astonishingly small.

A Very Short History

Perhaps the most important thing to say about the origins of sustainable residential designs is that they lie in ageless vernacular architecture, the kind of construction that was practiced for most of human history and continues to be practiced in what we in the West call the Third World. This approach relies on simple, renewable, and naturally insulating materials (such as adobe) and passive strategies like siting, thick walls, and natural ventilation to keep houses cool in summer and retain heat in winter. Roughly one-third of the world's population continues to live in such architecture. The lessons it offers for building environmentally responsible and energy-efficient housing remain as valuable and easy to copy as ever.

In a stylistic sense, to oversimplify at least a little, Western architecture has been drifting away from those traditions since the Greeks. Still, the divorce between architecture and the environment was not really finalized until the beginning of the twentieth century, when the modernists' love affair with new industrial technologies, from the elevator to steel-frame construction, produced an architecture that did its best to exist apart from nature. Indeed, by the early decades of the twentieth century the ideal piece of residential architecture had become a rectilinear, pure-white box set off in a field. The modernist master Le Corbusier called his version "a machine for living," a building that gained its undeniable charisma precisely from the way it was everything that the field was not: hard where the field was soft, monochromatic instead of multihued, closed instead of open, its edges factory-cut instead of weather-softened.

The critique of modernist architecture as anti-green is by now a familiar one, and we think it has sometimes been overstated. It is worth pointing out, for example, that modernism began with the same kind of reform-minded ethos that now drives green architecture—and that some of the figures who helped inspire the sustainability movement, Buckminster Fuller prominently among them, were believers in modernism who hoped to harness technology to improve the lives of the average family. As Kevin Pratt, an architect and critic based in London, has pointed out, "Green design speaks to a yearning for the kind of totalizing aesthetic and ideological program the modernists embraced. [It] also shares with the modernist project the righteousness of a cause: improving the world through reform of its material culture." In addition, a significant number of green landmarks over the last two decades have been designed by architects, like Britain's Hi Tech Group, whose approach and methodology grew directly from modernism. Pratt and other critics have gone so far as to predict that sustainability will be to the twenty-first century what modernism was to the twentieth—its dominant architectural movement. . . .

The term was brought into popular use by the Brundtland report, a 1987 United Nations document that defined sustainable development as meeting "the needs of the present without compromising the ability of future generations to meet their own." The concept provided architects with a sense of membership in an important larger effort, a way of defining precisely what they hoped to accomplish with their solar panels and walls made from recycled tires.

Even so, it took a while before the concept of sustainability merged vernacular elements with energy-efficient building practices to create what we now call green architecture. As a formal effort, the movement is younger than you might guess. As early as 1981 there were books like Robert Brown Butler's *The Ecological House* and proto-green developments like Davis,

California's Village Homes, but they were isolated efforts that predated any broad sense of eco-friendly architecture. Indeed, *The Green Reader*, a collection of essays published in 1991 that addressed sustainability in a wide variety of fields, did not mention architecture at all. But certainly by that year and soon after there were networks of architects who had begun to organize their practices around an ecologically sensitive approach to construction. The American Institute of Architects created its Committee on the Environment in 1992. The U.S. Green Building Council, a nonprofit association whose members include architects, developers, and builders, was founded in 1993. The first comprehensive books on the subject, such as Michael J. Crosbie's *Green Architecture: A Guide to Sustainable Design*, began appearing in bookstores over the following few years, and by the end of the millennium the term "green architecture" had seeped into the popular discourse.

A Movement's Priorities

As green architecture developed throughout the 1980s and 1990s, its leaders tended to pay little, if any, attention to the high design or academic corners of the architecture world. Instead, they rather stubbornly saw green design's priorities as higher-minded or simply more pressing than style or theory. They were determined to pay most of their attention (and perhaps quite rightly, given who makes the decisions about how and where to build, especially in the United States) to convincing corporate America that green design should be a mainstream rather than a marginal or eccentric pursuit.

In that battle they have made tremendous and undeniable progress. Sustainability advocates can finally say with confidence that the goals of green design have been embraced by a wide public. That public may be even wider than we suspect: Though they do not advertise this fact, even George W. Bush and his wife, Laura, have become patrons of green architecture. Their ranch house in Crawford, Texas, designed by Aus-

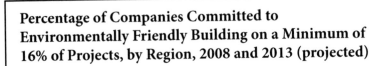

Percentage of Companies Committed to Environmentally Friendly Building on a Minimum of 16% of Projects, by Region, 2008 and 2013 (projected)

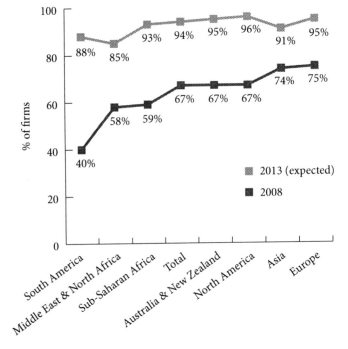

Source: McGraw Hill Construction, 2008

TAKEN FROM: Trade Queensland, "Green Building Opportunities: Global Demand," *Queensland Clean Technologies Exports*, vol. 1, no. 6, Spring 2009.

tin architect David Heymann and finished the same year Bush became president, has a number of sustainable features, including a system for recycling household water.

The Green Building Council's sustainable rating system for new buildings—known by its acronym LEED, for Leadership in Energy and Environmental Design—has achieved wide cultural currency since its formal introduction in 2000. It is not unusual now even for large corporate clients to push their architects to achieve a LEED rating because they know the public equates those standards with environmental responsibility. More than 1,000 buildings in the U.S. have earned LEED certification or are seeking it—roughly 5 percent of all commercial construction in this country, with that proportion surely bound to increase each year. (Already, roughly one in five institutional and government buildings are being built to LEED standards.) A LEED program for commercial interiors was launched in 2004, and one for residential architecture in 2005.

One of the biggest deterrents to sustainable building has been the perception of added expense. According to a study commissioned by the state of California, LEED buildings cost an average of $4 more per square foot than typical construction. But over twenty years, the study suggests, "they would generate savings of $48.87 a square foot (in current dollars) for standard- and silver-certified buildings, and $7.31 for gold- and platinum-certified buildings." To be fair, there is some guesswork involved in these projections; they rely on assumptions that green buildings will not only have lower operating costs than traditional ones but also that they will be more comfortable to work in, thereby increasing employee productivity.

Meanwhile, technological and manufacturing advances have made many green design features cheaper and easier to obtain than they had been. Solar panels designed to generate electricity, for example, cost about $100 per watt in the mid-1970s; they now sell for less than $3 per watt, and the price is continuing to fall. And new eco-friendly building materials appear on what seems a daily basis. Consider PV-TV, an inventive version of the solar panel developed in Japan. It can be used on the facade of a building in three ways at once: as a solar collector to generate electricity, as a transparent pane to allow sunlight into the interior, and as a screen to display video images.

As green architecture was gaining supporters in the political and commercial spheres, however, it was utterly failing to win them in the aesthetic realm. Sustainable building became associated in the public imagination with earnest, uninspired designs that put environmental concerns far ahead of artistic ones, creating what some critics dubbed the curse of "eco-banality." If in recent years you asked the average reader of an architecture or home-design magazine, say, to close her eyes and describe what came to mind at the mention of "green design" or "eco-architecture," she probably would have mentioned a sagging sod roof or a corporate office building with some energy-efficient features but little to recommend it architecturally. . . .

The Damage Done

Those architects' complaints about green design's lack of style, of course, were the design-world equivalent of fiddling while Rome burned. Indeed, for anyone who hasn't heard them before, the statistics on the amount of damage that the building industries do to the environment can be staggering. By one recent measure, buildings use 48 percent of all the energy consumed in the United States each year and are responsible for about half of American greenhouse gas emissions, which drive global warming. More than one-third of the material clogging U.S. landfills is produced by the construction and demolition of buildings. Worldwide, the numbers are not quite so bad but still drastically worse than they ought to be, and soaring population growth and rapid industrialization and urbanization in China, India, and elsewhere promises to wipe out the environmental progress being made in both the developed and developing world. Indeed, China now ranks second in the world, behind only the United States, as an emitter of greenhouse gases and is likely to take over the top spot on that dubious list within the next decade. And without a drastic global commitment to green architecture, the situation promises to get much worse. According to William Clark, a professor at Harvard's [John F.] Kennedy School of Government, "Over the next twenty to forty years, by any of the prevailing demographic calculations, there will be more urban built environment created than in all prior history."

Much of the environmental damage is the indirect result, many green design advocates say, of an architecture that has increasingly alienated its users from the natural world. "Our culture has adopted a design stratagem that essentially says that if brute force or massive amounts of energy don't work, you're not using enough of it," says the architect William McDonough, among the best-known practitioners of sustainable architecture.

> We made glass buildings that are more about buildings than they are about people. The hope that glass would connect us to the outdoors was completely stultified by making the buildings sealed. We have created stress in people because we are meant to be connected with the outdoors, but instead we are trapped. . . . People are sensing how horrifying it can be to be trapped indoors, especially with the thousands upon thousands of chemicals that are being used to make things today.

Green design experts have pointed out that most contemporary architecture is connected to globalization of the most destructive order. "Phillipine forests are clear-cut for plywood used to build offices in Japan," notes the Rocky Mountain Institute's *A Primer on Sustainable Building*.

> Homes in Southern California are framed with old-growth lumber from Washington and powered by burning coal strip-mined from Navajo sacred lands in Arizona. Ultimately, the costs of poor design are borne not solely by a building's owner and those who work and live there, but by everyone.

In the face of such statistics, it is easy to despair about the possibility of a turnaround, especially one led by architecture—and, more specifically, by residential architecture. After all, the number of private homes designed by architects each year around the world is tiny compared to the many buildings, from housing developments to office parks, that are constructed without the benefit of a design professional. What's more, those designed by the architects on the cutting edge of the profession would seem to have little direct connection to the kind of suburban tract houses produced on a massive scale.

But architecture is a field, like fashion, where style, and even avant-garde style, matters more and more and is separated from the man on the street less and less with each passing year. Architects and builders alike—even those without fancy reputations—read the architecture and design press as surely as merchandisers for Target or Macy's follow what is on the runway in Milan or Paris. Since the 1997 opening of Frank Gehry's branch of the Guggenheim Museum in Bilbao, Spain, there has been a much-touted explosion of interest in design and architecture, and new connections have been forged between high-design architecture and the public at large. Even before it opened in 2003 in downtown Los Angeles, Gehry's Walt Disney Concert Hall was appearing in car ads in glossy magazines—surely proof, if any were still needed, that contemporary architecture is no longer estranged from popular culture.

Meanwhile, the number of well-known or avant-garde architects whose firms have been pursuing sustainable design in good faith has been growing. This group now includes such luminaries as Renzo Piano, Sir Norman Foster, Glenn Murcutt, and Herzog & de Meuron, all of whom have won the Pritzker [Architecture] Prize, architecture's version of the Nobel. Santiago Calatrava, designer of the critically acclaimed new transit hub for the World Trade Center site in lower Manhattan, lent his skills to a progressive sustainable neighborhood in Malmö, Sweden. What all of this means for the green design movement is simple: not only do architects have a celebrity status that they did not possess a decade ago, but even their experimental work has become part of mainstream culture. The fact that many famous architects are turning to green architecture suggests sustainability will gain exposure, in the media and elsewhere, that it might not receive otherwise.

It is also encouraging that technological progress, so long the enemy of the natural world, is increasingly being put in the service of saving and restoring nature—and that this new partnership is producing some of its most significant dividends in the realm of architecture, where modeling programs, to pick one example, now help designers measure the efficiency of their buildings with remarkable accuracy while they are still on the computer screen. As a result, green architects of all kinds are ditching their old reputation as regressive Luddites [those opposed to technological change] who were content to labor in isolation from cultural—and architectural—developments.

| "The three main types of benefits associated with sustainable construction are environmental, economic and health and community benefits."

Eco-Architecture Is Economically Beneficial

DNA: Daily News & Analysis

DNA: Daily News & Analysis is an Indian broadsheet published in English. In the following viewpoint, the author proposes that green buildings offer numerous advantages to businesses. In addition to reduced energy and operating costs, green buildings have the potential for greater durability and enhanced occupant comfort or health. The article claims that sustainability is becoming a main driver of growth and value creation.

As you read, consider the following questions:

1. According to the article, what is a "Green Economy"?

2. As stated in the viewpoint, what should be the main focus of building green?

3. What is becoming one of the main drivers of value creation?

The 2012 theme for World Environment Day is Green Economy: Does it include you? Practically speaking, a Green Economy is one whose growth in income and employment is driven by public and private investments that reduce carbon emissions and pollution, enhance energy and resource efficiency, and prevent the loss of biodiversity and ecosystem services.

Since sustainability in construction plays an important role in this, there are certain logical questions that arise. What are the key aspects that need to be taken into account where the 'green building' concept is concerned? How can these be made more affordable and utilised in a greater number of new buildings being planned? What are the practical benefits driving the growing shift towards eco-friendly construction solutions?

Green Means Positive

Elaborating on these concepts, Prasad Chandran, chairman, BASF Companies in India and head South Asia, explains, "Green Buildings mean providing meaningful, measureable, positive benefits to lower emissions, usage of energy, materials, water, labour, health and enhance safety over the life cycle of a structure, while meeting or exceeding the building performance. The essence of optimal usage of resources is closely linked to the philosophy of lean design which is being applied to construction processes, aimed at minimizing waste and also reducing the gap between design and construction.

"Therefore, the main focus should be on balancing the ecological, economic and social aspects during design, execution, operation and disposal of building structure and surroundings. This will contribute to the purpose of long-term sustainability in the construction space, promoting the 'green' concept."

According to him, there is a growing momentum in both the public and private sectors for [a] more sustainable approach towards building construction. Influencing factors are

Breakthrough Opportunity for Green Design

As the economic benefits of green and energy-efficient buildings become apparent to more developers and builders, the demand for advice and consulting on technologies and processes is skyrocketing among builders large and small. That's a great business opportunity for entrepreneurs and job seekers with expertise in green architecture, design, and engineering. The financial payoff from green building will be multifaceted, comprising direct savings from reduced energy use, higher value in the real estate market (including resale value), increased employee retention and productivity, and potential carbon credits from reduced CO_2 emissions. So a wide variety of skill sets can be brought to bear. There'll be demand for firms and individuals with expertise in very specific areas, such as the latest window glazing or HVAC [heating, ventilation, and air-conditioning] improvements, as well as those skilled in green-building project management and accountability.

Ron Pernick and Clint Wilder, The Clean Tech Revolution: The Next Big Growth and Investment Opportunity, New York: HarperCollins, 2007.

the need to reduce raw materials, water and energy use, and waste and greenhouse gases output. However, even more important than mitigating these negative impacts is the potential of amplifying the positive impacts of occupant satisfaction and performance and durability of green buildings.

Benefits of Sustainable Construction

The three main types of benefits associated with sustainable construction are environmental, economic and health and community benefits. Environmental benefits include improved air and water quality, reduced energy and water consumption and reduced waste disposal. Economic benefits include reduced operational costs, reduced maintenance costs and durability of the buildings. Health and community benefits encompass enhanced occupant comfort or health and indoor air-quality enabling more productive work or living space. Overall green construction would also reduce the stress on resources created by [a] growing population, need for urbanisation and work towards conserving the environment.

For instance, construction chemicals are less than 1% of the overall building cost. In some cases, materials with a longer life span can require a somewhat higher initial investment, although usually not more than 5–7% higher than average. However, in the long run it turns out to be much cheaper, with longer life span, better durability, more resistance to weathering and reduction in energy consumption.

In this perspective, we can also draw reference to the automotive industry in terms of implementing modular or mass production. Currently, construction industry players are too focused on individual design of buildings. Instead, modular design would facilitate mass production of the components and make it more affordable and accelerate the speed of construction, he feels.

More and more people are now moving to live in cities. By 2050 it is estimated that the population will grow to about nine billion, with 75% being urban dwellers. This is uncharted territory and it requires new concepts for housing and construction. Global construction is facing the challenge of supporting a good quality of life for people in an increasingly urbanized world while at the same time improving resource conservation and cost efficiency.

Chemistry enables speed, durability, aesthetics, improved indoor air quality, reduced mass for construction and usage of natural resources. It enables affordability while maintaining high aesthetics and consistent quality.

Sustainability is becoming one of the main drivers of growth and value creation. It can only be achieved through innovation and that is where chemistry plays an essential role. Innovations for sustainable construction, for example, require a wider portfolio, better understanding of local industry, its need, growth potential and a thorough understanding of the customers' value chains. Further, it can help reduce costs and thereby clear the myth that green building solutions are expensive and increase overall construction cost. Local innovations make the concept of green buildings more acceptable and thereby accelerate business growth, he emphasises.

> "Because many green building products
> and techniques are unfamiliar, the risk
> is even greater."

Eco-Architecture Is Economically Risky

Teresa Burney

In the following viewpoint, Teresa Burney contends that green construction comes with a higher likelihood of liability and unforeseen costs for builders. Sustainable building products are new and unfamiliar, she states, adding to the potential pitfalls and responsibilities of traditional construction. Also, the author outlines five ways sustainable building practices result in additional expenses and lawsuits from consumers: construction is not strictly guided or monitored; "green" and "sustainable" are used as misleading marketing terms; claims of building products and promises for certification fall short; consumer expectations are too high and unmet; and claims of building products are fraudulent. Burney is senior editor of Builder *magazine.*

As you read, consider the following questions:

1. Why can't a "truly green house" be built quickly, according to Burney?

2. How can a builder construct a home that is green certified but does not meet the expectations of the consumer, as stated by the author?

3. As described by the author, what happened in the case of a green building that promised "healthier and more productive occupants" but had employees whoreported more illnesses and less productivity?

In a heartbeat, Tom Hoyt, cofounder of McStain Neighborhoods, recalls a striking example of how painful and costly missteps in building green homes at a high volume can be.

Back in the mid-1990s, the Denver, Colo.-based company decided to install cutting-edge heating systems in its Indian Peaks community outside of Denver. McStain chose what was then a state-of-the-art, high-efficiency heating system for the homes. Designed for multifamily communities, it was a ducted, forced-air system that derived heat from a hot water heater via a heat exchange coil.

The problem was, in a multifamily installation, the system used a large boiler as opposed to a typical residential hot water heater. In the single-family application, water heaters of the time were not capable of providing sufficient BTU [British thermal unit] values consistently.

"It was a poor piece of engineering," says Hoyt. "We had 189 of them installed before we realized it."

By then, there was no chance of retrofitting the systems to make them perform better. Homeowners wanted heat, not necessarily technology. To preserve the company's reputation, McStain replaced all the hot water systems with conventional, gas-fired, forced-air furnaces that were both efficient and proven over time.

Lesson learned. Now McStain experiments with new technology on one or two homes at a time, creating real-life beta tests for innovations and new products.

Problems with Innovation

"Really, it's a shame how much the liability world stifles innovation," says Hoyt, an architect by training who has been working to build sustainable "green" houses for 40 years. "You need to be so careful." It's a lesson attorneys, those who advise builders about liability and keep an eye out on trends in liability claims, are working to inculcate in the many newbie builders jumping on the green building bandwagon.

When production home builders pick the wrong product and install it on a big scale, the cost of a misstep is exponential. Because many green building products and techniques are unfamiliar, the risk is even greater. Then add on the risk associated with exposure to liability on new products.

"You have all the normal risks and responsibilities that always exist [in home construction], plus some new elements in terms of methodologies, requirements, and products," says Keith McGlamery of Ballard Spahr Andrews & Ingersoll, one of 100 LEED accredited attorneys in the country. "Any time you add that many new elements, you can have some confusion and the possibility of error. . . . You increase the stakes dramatically."

The stakes get even higher during an economic downturn, like the one seen in the housing and financial markets in 2008.

"As economic conditions worsen, there is less margin for error," says McGlamery. "Budgets are restricted and suppliers, subcontractors, and so forth may have financial difficulties; there are certainly lots of impacts on the project, and sometimes those impacts can put a project or developer in such peril that they end up in litigation."

While the risks may be great, the potential rewards of differentiating your product from others are as well, says Hoyt.

"The worse [the market] gets, the more convinced I am that our platform, where we have really focused on trying to be the leading edge of production green, is the place to be when we come out of this," he says. "When the market comes back, it's going to be a different market."

"Green building is happening now," says Jay B. Freedman, a construction litigation specialist with Newport Beach, Calif.-based Newmeyer & Dillion LLP. "The goal is to make sure it's done right.... I think the industry is going to educate itself over the next three years."

Green Building Pitfalls

In the meantime, here are five places where attorneys experienced in green building practices and pitfalls say builders seeking to go green can go seriously astray.

1—Piecemeal Green "The No. 1 way of preventing problems is to go with green building from the very beginning of a project and [ensure] the entire team—all of the players, including the vendors, suppliers, and designers—are aware so everyone understands what their role is and how it fits into achieving green certification," says McGlamery. "It's both expensive and more difficult if you decide partway through the project to go green."

That's because a truly green house can't be cobbled together on the fly. Its design and construction take into account every aspect of the house, from where it's built and how it sits on the lot to the materials used in its construction and how they work together. More than a collection of sustainable parts, it is a series of systems that work together to create a high-performance machine. Replacing, altering, or failing to correctly install any links in that chain can create a house that isn't green.

"Putting Energy Star appliances in a house with glazing on the windows that allows the house to roast in the afternoon and cause you to run the air-conditioning 24-7 [won't make a house green]," McGlamery says.

The integration and education of the entire team, from site development through sales can't be overemphasized, lawyers say. Every team member should know the role they are playing to make the house sustainable and environmentally friendly, even to the point of specifying it in their contracts.

McGlamery offers an example from a commercial office project that shows what can happen when even one part of the team isn't clear on its duties.

An office building that had promised tenants LEED certification was nearing completion and a major tenant was days from moving in when the painter ran out of paint, and his supplier was out of the low-VOC [volatile organic compounds] paint required for the LEED rating. So the painter, concerned only with matching the paint's color, finished the job with paint that was't low-VOC. That one act disqualified the building from receiving the certification, and the tenant, promised a building with a certain certification, threatened to sue.

"If you think about it, that painting subcontractor probably had one of the smallest contracts on the project," says McGlamery. Yet his decision probably cost the developer many times the value of his contract.

Because some green products require exacting or unusual installation methods that could lead to failure if done incorrectly, it's imperative to make sure the trades receive training on the techniques with emphasis that the installation needs to be done correctly every time.

"Builders just can't do green projects on a business-as-usual basis," explains Newmeyer & Dillion's Freedman.

2—Green Undefined Many litigators suggest that builders refrain from using the word "green" when marketing their houses and neighborhoods.

"It doesn't mean anything yet, or it means too many things," says Freedman. "My personal advice would be to market what the green features are, such as if you have installed a tankless water heater. . . . Market what's there that's a fact."

David Crump, director of legal research for NAHB [National Association of Home Builders], agrees. "There are a lot of general, undefined terms associated with green building, and there is no common standard definition of what those mean."

Crump suggests ditching the standard construction contract and defining the terms to eliminate the potential for misunderstanding. "You are going to have to define what you mean by green, whether it's a green certification or sustainability, so there's no confusion on what you are providing under the contract."

Another reason to avoid the terms "green" and "sustainable" is that they have attracted the attention of the Federal Trade Commission as well as the consumer protection arms of state governments, increasing the chances that those agencies will clamp down on companies that advertise their products as green without proof, says Crump.

3—Making Promises Promising a healthier home or a certain amount of energy savings is risky as well. "Those claims are very difficult to quantify, and the actual experience of individual purchasers will vary depending on the individuals' lifestyle and the climatic region they live in," says Crump. "It's not a good idea."

And those who do make such claims should include disclaimers explaining that results can—and likely will—vary.

"Once the house is constructed and placed in the hands of a homeowner, you don't know what they are going to do," Crump says. "Also, maintenance has a lot to do with the continued performance of green construction. . . . Unless you have the assurance that the house will be maintained to a certain standard, you can't be sure the house will perform at that level."

"If you represent that people who occupy your building will have substantially fewer respiratory illnesses or that it's a much healthier environment, you had better be able to back it up," adds McGlamery. "If you claim that your project is much more energy efficient, then you had better be able to back it up. More energy efficient than what?"

Promising that a house will meet a third-party green certification is tricky, too. "What is going to happen if you don't get it?" Crump asks.

A lawsuit is one possibility. "Fraud claims or negligent representation claims, none of that is covered by insurance," says Freedman. "They could say, 'You told me this house would be healthier, and my kid is still sick,' or, 'You told me that this house would use less energy.'" Builders who make such promises should probably set aside greater reserves to handle claims that might come up, Freedman says.

4—High Hopes Builders can get in trouble for what they imply as well as what they promise. Consumers often have high expectations from homes marketed as green and are disappointed if the house isn't what they thought it would be. "The homeowner may end up suing because they didn't get what they expected—even if they weren't promised it," says McGlamery.

Because there's no universal definition of "green" or "sustainable" and there are several ways to achieve certification, there's a strong possibility that a consumer might think the builder is going to deliver something different from what they get.

"Without a definition, a consumer is going to have a much higher expectation of what that home is going to be," notes Jeffrey D. Masters, a real estate litigator and partner at Cox, Castle & Nicholson in Los Angeles. "They might expect a house free of any defects, or think they don't have to maintain the home because it's green. Or the owner may have an expectation that they will save money on their energy bills, and that expectation might not be realized."

A builder might guarantee to deliver a house that is green certified under a given program while the consumer assumes it will be energy efficient or healthier. However, since certification programs often are based on point systems, the builder may have accumulated all the points through using drought-resistant landscaping, lumber from sustainable forests, and recycled materials, according to Masters. "We really have to manage expectations," he says.

Freedman suggests that sales managers ask customers what they expect from their home and write it down in case litigation should come later.

"Find out what the buyers are looking for, and if that's not what you've got, manage the expectations so everyone knows what's happening," he says.

5—Believing Pretty Lies "Green" has become one of the most popular words to slap on product marketing materials. Sometimes the claim is true, sometimes it's somewhat true, and sometimes it's an "absolute, flat-out lie," says Freedman. "They say it's an environmentally conscious product when it isn't."

It's the builder's responsibility to make sure what they sell as "green" actually is. "If the claim ultimately proves to be false, they could be liable," says Crump, even if the builder was unaware the claim was false.

"Who says it's green, and why?" Freedman asks. Another question to ask: Is there third-party certification?

All the new, untested "green" products and techniques introduced at once make lawyers nervous because there is no assurance they will perform well long term, not to mention the possibility that new products could create problems with other products.

"These products weren't available two or three years ago," says McGlamery. "It may be that the product doesn't perform as expected, so there is a problem of redesigning or retrofitting or replacement. And who bears the cost of that?"

For instance, one technique for some climates has builders turning attics into heated/cooled spaces by using spray foam insulation on the roof sheathing. "If you have a roof leak along that insulation, it could take longer to see it and the water could spread," suggests Freedman.

Builders need to be careful that they do not warranty products, and that whatever guarantees are offered go directly to the manufacturer, says Crump.

Performance aside, "you need to make sure that the design professional knows of its availability," adds McGlamery. "If you are dependent on bamboo flooring, make sure there's an adequate amount deliverable in the time frame that you need so it doesn't impact the building schedule."

And sometimes a product is green and of high quality, but it doesn't perform well in a given space or is installed improperly.

While all the legal caveats are enough to discourage even the most gung ho builder, Freedman has some words of encouragement. "Hopefully by building green we are actually building better. Building green is just building right. As we build better, there should be a decrease in litigation."

Green May Yield Broken Promises

Unfulfilled green can lead to red flags and big money.

Nobody really knows how many or what kind of lawsuits green home building will spark. Because the process is so new in residential construction and since many cases are settled quietly out of court, it will most likely be years before patterns emerge. Yet there is a canary in the coal mine—professional liability claims against design firms working in the more mature field of commercial green construction. Attorneys who advise home builders say they can make a sound guess as to what will get home builders in trouble from considering those cases. Below are summaries of claims made against design professionals related to green construction from Frank Musica, senior risk management attorney for Victor O. Schinnerer & Co., a provider of educational programs and management assistance to design firms and contractors with liability insurance.

An architect agreed to design a LEED gold office building. The developer advertised the building as boasting "reduced operating costs and healthier and more productive occupants" to attract tenants at higher rents. Budget and time constraints prevented the building from achieving the certification, and the developer sued the architect for negligence, breach of contract, and breach of warranty based on the architect's "guarantee" of gold certification.

A developer received approval for a project based on promises of tightly constrained water use. The design team utilized water conservation systems including rainwater collection and gray water use. Adjoining landowners sued, saying the rainwater collection system violated state law regulating natural water flow. Without the rainwater, the project's water use exceeded the limit agreed to by the developer, forcing it to pay fines. The developer sued the design team for negligence, as well as breach of contract and warranty due to the extra water use.

A design firm used a new green product with impressive promotional information, conducting no research on whether the product would be available and failing to warn the owner of potential problems related to supply. Based on design firm recommendation, the owner agreed to its use. When the product was not readily available, the project was delayed and construction schedule distorted. The contractor demanded more money for overhead, lost profits, and out-of-sequence construction. The owner sued the design firm, as he wasn't informed product delivery would be delayed.

A homeowner asked an architect for a low-cost addition that would provide a healthy interior and save on energy costs. The architect agreed, discussing expertise and how design and service would "assure" satisfaction with an on-time and within-budget project. The owner, unhappy with cost, time, and results, sued the architect under consumer protection laws, alleging fraud in the inducement to the contract for services, and demanded rescission of contract and return of fee and legal costs, even though the project was complete.

Lured by the promise of "healthier and more productive occupants" basic to LEED publicity, a tenant rented space in a silver certified building. At the end of the year, the tenant's records indicated greater use of sick leave, increased employee complaints of eye strain and drafts, and reduced output by clerical staff. The tenant demanded rent rebate based on a false promise of a healthy workplace and increased productivity. The owner sued the architect for not designing a healthy workplace. The tenant then sued the architect for bodily injury based on poor indoor air quality.

A green design included "environmentally friendly" sealants to achieve a green designation. The subcontractor used the wrong sealant, then later argued the sealant had been improperly specified and, even if properly specified, would not have worked. The sealant had to be removed but already had off-gassed. The subcontractor declared bankruptcy. The client brought a claim against the architect based on improper specification and negligent construction observation.

A design team agreed to a three-school project to serve as an example of sustainable design and energy conservation. The architects and consulting engineers signed a contract that stated the projects would "reduce operating costs by 50 percent" over schools of similar size. But the schools' energy use was comparable to other schools recently designed and built. The school system was publicly embarrassed and blamed for being "hoodwinked" by the architect and engineers. The school system brought a claim against them.

> *"Although climate change considerations spurred the LEED-era green building movement, the health of these buildings may be the primary impetus for the demand that drives the continued shift within the real estate industry."*

The LEED Building Standards Protect Human Health

Shannon D. Sentman

In the following viewpoint, Shannon D. Sentman argues that sick building syndrome (SBS), in which occupants' illnesses or conditions correlate to time spent in a building, has become prevalent, and the US Green Building Council's Leadership in Energy and Environmental Design (LEED) standards effectively address unhealthy workplace conditions. In a LEED-certified building, indoor air quality and use of natural light are improved, he maintains, and numerous studies demonstrate that these benefits can reduce sick leave and increase productivity among occupants. Based in Washington, DC, Sentman is a LEED-accredited attorney and strategic consultant; he is adjunct professor for the Colvin Institute of Real Estate Development at the University of Maryland.

Shannon D. Sentman, "Healthy Buildings: Green Building Standards, Benefits, and Incentives," *Journal of Israel Innovation* (Special Supplement: Israel Edition of *Journal of Biolaw and Business*, vol. 12, no. 1, 2009). Reproduced by permission.

As you read, consider the following questions:

1. In Sentman's view, how does sick building syndrome impact a business's bottom line?

2. What six areas does LEED address, as described by Sentman?

3. How much can American businesses save by making improvements to indoor air quality, according to the Lawrence Berkeley National Laboratory?

With the [President Bill] Clinton years [1993–2001] waning and George W. Bush poised to take his place as the 43rd president of the United States, few could foresee the forthcoming shift in the real estate industry. Fewer still would have guessed that the man who lost the election to soon-to-be President Bush would be a key player in this shift. That man, of course, was former vice president Al Gore, whose star swept the U.S. and the world as he marched with a single-minded determination to educate the masses of the calamity that befell our natural environment if the world's people and governments failed to address climate change. Mr. Gore placed the blame for climate change squarely on human-caused greenhouse gas (GHG) emissions, and, according to Mr. Gore, addressing this issue meant altering human behavior to reduce these emissions.

As the principal culprits for GHG emissions, the sectors of industry, transportation, and buildings came into sharp focus. In the U.S., of these three sectors, buildings are responsible for the highest level of GHG emissions—39% of the nation's total. These emissions result from the energy consumed by building, which includes 70% of the electricity produced in the U.S. and 40% of the nation's total energy.

The new green consciousness spurred by Mr. Gore impacted the commercial real estate industry from several angles. For one, local governments, impatient with the lack of a federal response to climate change, began creating incentives to encourage the development of green buildings, while also passing mandates to force the development of green buildings. At the same time, market demand for green buildings began to swell. Exposed to these factors, and in the midst of an unprecedented boom, the commercial real estate industry saw green buildings grow from a niche market to a major segment of the industry.

Although former vice president Gore's central mission was to reduce GHG emissions, there was a side effect to his actions. Many in the real estate industry, and many real estate users, began to take a closer look at the impact of green buildings on the health and productivity of occupants of these buildings. With stories of "sick buildings" becoming more prevalent, the industry began to realize that green buildings are healthy buildings, and the companies occupying these buildings were receiving a financial benefit in the form of enhanced worker health and productivity. This benefit, along with other more tangible bottom-line benefits, is a key factor in overcoming the biggest hurdle to green building—the increased costs associated with these projects, known as the "green premium."

As businesses better understand the benefits of green buildings, the demand for greener buildings will continue the shift that is already well under way in the real estate market. To understand why this shift will continue, even in the face of a green premium, requires an understanding of green buildings and how they compare to conventional buildings.

Sick Building Syndrome

Most have heard the term "sick building syndrome" (SBS), but few understand what it means. This lack of understanding is akin to terms like "soft-tissue damage," and often met with the similar skepticism. The skepticism results from the anomalous nature of sick building syndrome. As defined by the Environmental Protection Agency [EPA], the term "sick building syndrome" describes "situations in which building occupants experience acute health and comfort effects that appear to be linked to time spent in a building, but no specific illness or cause can be identified."

Despite any skepticism that may exist, institutions like the World Health Organization and the U.S. Environmental Protection Agency view sick building syndrome as a serious problem. According to a report released in 1984 by the World Health Organization, up to 30% of new and remodeled buildings worldwide may be the subject of excessive complaints related to indoor air quality (IAQ), which is the primary culprit for sick building syndrome. Combine this with consideration of the amount of time adult Americans spend indoors—90% of their time according to the EPA—and the problem becomes clearer.

For businesses, sick building syndrome can impact the bottom line in numerous ways—increased absenteeism, liability for ailments, increased health costs, lost productivity, etc. According to the EPA publication "An Office Building Occupant's Guide to Indoor Air Quality," "poor indoor air may cost the nation tens of billions of dollars each year in lost productivity and medical care."

Green Buildings, Healthy Buildings

When defining what makes a building "green," indoor air quality is one of several factors considered. Generally, green buildings, as distinguished from their conventional peers, are developed and operated to minimize negative impacts on the natural environment, and on building occupants. In addition to improved indoor air quality, other key attributes of green buildings include environmentally sensitive siting, efficient use of natural resources, and increased use of natural light.

Because the general/conceptual definition of green buildings does not offer a threshold distinction from conventional buildings, the real estate industry has struggled to distinguish real green buildings from those employing "green" merely as a marketing tool. To resolve this issue, various groups developed green building standards in hopes of creating a common definition.

Green Building Standards

Unlike most building standards, which typically focus on specific aspects of a building (*i.e.* indoor air quality, energy efficiency, fire safety, etc.), green building standards are comprehensive in nature, taking many aspects of a building's development and operation into consideration. In fact, many green building standards or ratings systems are actually a compilation of a number of specific standards. Unlike green building standards, building standards like Energy Star, which focuses solely on energy efficiency, do not look at a building holistically. While energy efficiency is important for green buildings, absent consideration of indoor air quality and other environmental impacts, energy efficiency alone does not necessarily make a building green.

Although numerous green building standards exist in the U.S. and abroad, the clear leader in the domestic commercial real estate market is the Leadership in Energy and Environmental Design (LEED) green building rating system developed by the United States Green Building Council (USGBC). Founded in 1993, USGBC is a nonprofit trade organization whose membership consists primarily of building industry stakeholders with a mission to promote sustainable design, construction, and operation throughout the real estate industry.

Five years after its founding, USGBC released the LEED 1.0 pilot program. In developing this first version of LEED, early council members (informed by existing green building standards—UK's BREEAM [Building Research Establishment Environmental Assessment Method] and Canada's BEPAC

[Building Environmental Performance Assessment Criteria]—endeavored to create a custom, voluntary system for U.S. buildings. Ultimately, the goal in creating LEED was to stimulate market demand for greener buildings. By most standards, LEED has achieved this goal. As of February 18, 2009, there were 2,271 LEED certified buildings worldwide, with another 17,723 buildings registered for certification.

The success of the LEED rating system is due in part to the constant refinement of the system. Since its inception, the LEED rating system has not only grown from one standard for new construction to a comprehensive system covering almost the full gamut of project types, it has also seen numerous versions of the criteria underlying many of the various systems.

Despite this refinement, the six major areas that LEED addresses remain consistent—sustainable sites, water efficiency, energy and atmosphere, materials and resources, indoor environmental quality, and innovation in design process. The first five of these six areas are the environmental categories, with the latter acting primarily as a catchall for sustainable practices otherwise unaddressed by the other categories.

Within each of the categories are various criteria classified as either prerequisites or credits. Although the criteria differ depending on the specific LEED rating system applicable to a given project, certification under each system requires that the project satisfy all of the prerequisites plus a threshold number of credits. For each credit that a project achieves, it earns a certain number of points toward certification. If a project earns the minimum threshold of points, USGBC awards the project with certification. To provide incentive to projects that push beyond the minimum certification requirements, USGBC awards projects one of four rating levels—certified, silver, gold, or platinum—each more onerous than the prior. The total number of points that a project earns is the basis for the rating level awarded. USGBC recognizes LEED-rated buildings with a mountable plaque.

Green Premium

Undoubtedly, the single biggest hurdle to a market-wide shift to developing green buildings has been the perceived high cost of designing and constructing these buildings as compared to their conventional peers. This perception is, at least in part, a relic of the early years of the LEED era of green building (the late '90s and early in this decade), when green building developers often paid high premiums for projects due to, among other things, lack of experience and knowledge among the building professions and the high costs of "green" building materials from niche manufacturers.

As experience among the professions grew and green building materials became readily available on the mass market, the cost of developing green projects decreased rapidly. The results of numerous studies comparing the cost of green building to conventional building show the "green premium" as ranging from 0 to 10%, with most buildings falling below a two percent increase as compared to a conventional building. In a frequently cited 2003 study by Gregory H. Kats, the green premium for the various LEED certification levels of 33 buildings were as follows: 0.66% for LEED certified, 2.11% for LEED silver, 1.82% for LEED gold, and 6.5% for LEED platinum. This translated to a total increase of $3.00–$5.00 per square foot. Further, a 2006 study of 221 buildings by Davis Langdon concluded, "there is no significant difference in average costs for green buildings as compared to non-green buildings."

Despite these studies, the perception of the "green premium" remains high among many in the real estate industry. In a 2007 survey by Building Design & Construction, 41% of the responding architects, engineers, contractors, and developers/owners believed the overall cost of green building was 11% or more above the cost of conventional building.

Although the perception of the green premium may be exaggerated, most green building advocates will admit that green

Sick Building Syndrome

According to a groundbreaking Swedish study appearing in the *International Archives of Occupational and Environmental Health*, 45% of so-called 'Sick Building Syndrome' (SBS) victims—treated at hospital clinics—no longer have the capacity to work. Twenty percent of these sufferers are receiving disability pensions, 25% are "on the sick list." Emphasizing SBS's devastating potential, the study warned that the possibility "of having no work capabilities at follow-up was significantly increased if the time from (SBS) onset to first visit at the hospital clinic was more than 1 year. This risk was also significantly higher if the patient at the first visit had five or more symptoms."

Ritt Goldstein, "Sick Building Syndrome: Floods, Mold, Cancer, and the Politics of Public Health," CommonDreams.org, March 30, 2009. www.commondreams.org.

projects do cost at least marginally more to develop than their conventional counterparts. Because most building owners must answer to financing sources—lenders, investors, stockholders, taxpayers, etc.—projects are unlikely to include such increased green investments unless the market shows them as prudent. For the market to show them as prudent typically requires higher tenant demand for these buildings and higher rents.

Return on Green

Additional investment in green features is prudent when the benefits of these features offset any green premium—*i.e.* the return on investment justifies the increased initial investment. Applying the findings from the Kats study, for most projects, the required return on investment must justify a premium of $3.00–$5.00 per square foot. The benefits most frequently cited as resulting in increased returns for green buildings include decreased operating expenses resulting from reduced consumption of energy and water, reduced waste, insurance savings, enhanced worker productivity and health, decreased capital investment requirements due to available incentives, decreased risk of governmental policy impact, expedited construction permitting and entitlement procedures in some localities, and increased operating revenue due to higher rent, increased occupancy, and net metering.

Of these benefits, decreased operating expenses are the most tangible. In his 2003 study, Kats estimated that the commissioning associated with LEED certified buildings, together with reduced consumption of energy and water, results in a savings of $1.16 per square foot annually, for a 20-year present value of $14.77 per square foot based on a 5% discount rate. This alone seems to justify the $3.00–$5.00 per square foot premium.

In addition to operating savings, which are easily quantified with standard building valuation metrics, green building advocates taut the less quantifiable benefits of green buildings as their real selling point. These include increased worker retention and enhanced productivity, health and well-being, resulting in reduced health care and insurance costs. Numerous studies support this point, showing that the improved indoor air quality and the increased natural light associated with green buildings make for better work environments. From the standpoint of the average building user, the cost of facilities (renting/owning and operating real estate) accounts for only a small percentage of overall company expenses, in comparison to personnel-related costs. Given the cost of personnel, any enhancements resulting from green buildings likely justify higher rents.

To support the proposition that green buildings enhance worker productivity and health, a study by Lawrence Berkeley National Laboratory concluded that American businesses could save as much as $58 billion in lost sick time and $200 billion in workers' performance by making improvements to indoor air quality. Additionally, studies by Herman Miller [Inc.] found worker productivity increased by up to 7% in green, day-lit facilities. Essentially, these and numerous other studies support the proposition that green buildings are the counterpoint to those buildings blamed for sick building syndrome. Altogether, these benefits also purportedly result in greater worker loyalty and retention for the "green" employer.

In valuing the personnel-related benefits of green buildings, Kats estimated that a mere 1% increase in productivity (approximately 5 minutes per day) for an employee receiving annual compensation of $66,478.00 results in a productivity gain of approximately $665.00 per employee, or $2.96 per square foot annually. Applying Kats' life-cycle analysis, improved personnel health and productivity result in a 20-year present value of $36.89 per square foot for LEED certified and silver buildings and $55.33 for LEED gold and platinum buildings.

Green Buildings Incentives

In addition to operating benefits, owners developing green buildings and tenants occupying green buildings may benefit from local, state, and federal incentives. All 50 states, the federal government, and many local jurisdictions offer various incentives for energy efficiency, renewable energy, or specifically for green buildings. To name a few, these incentives come in the form of tax credits and deductions, grants, low-cost loans, reduced property taxes, expedited permitting, and reduced fees. Due to appropriations and other issues, many view these incentive programs with due caution....

Although climate change considerations spurred the LEED-era green building movement, the health of these buildings may be the primary impetus for the demand that drives the continued shift within the real estate industry. In light of liabilities associated with "sick buildings" and benefits associated with healthy buildings, conscientious owners and tenants should continue to move away from conventional offerings.

"The nation needs a comprehensive federal law to control the chemical content of the built environment. LEED is simply not up to the job."

The LEED Building Standards Do Not Protect Human Health

John Wargo

Leadership in Energy and Environmental Design (LEED) is a voluntary set of building standards developed by the US Green Building Council. In the following viewpoint, John Wargo asserts that LEED increases a building's energy efficiency but does not account for human health. According to him, LEED approves the use of chemicals—many unregulated—that are recognized as hazardous or toxic. Moreover, airtight, energy-saving, LEED-certified buildings trap these harmful substances and gases in indoor air, increasing occupants' exposure, Wargo alleges. He recommends that federal regulation address the shortcomings of the rating system. The author is a professor at the Yale School of Forestry and Environmental Studies, chair of the environmental studies major at Yale, and advisor to the US Centers for Disease Control and Prevention.

As you read, consider the following questions:

1. How does LEED certification ignore indoor air quality in its point and credit system, as told by Wargo?

2. What chemicals does LEED approve in buildings, as provided by the author?

3. Why does LEED focus primarily on energy conservation, according to Wargo?

The LEED program—Leadership in Energy and Environmental Design—is playing an increasingly important role in the drive to make buildings in the United States greener and more energy efficient. LEED is now the most prominent and widely adopted green building certification program in the country, with architects and developers striving to earn LEED's coveted platinum or gold rating, and an increasing number of local, state, and federal regulations beginning to incorporate LEED standards into official building codes.

Indoor Air Pollution in Green Buildings

But LEED—sponsored by the U.S. Green Building Council, an industry group—has a glaring and little-known drawback: It places scant emphasis on factors relating to human health, even as the largely unregulated use of potentially toxic building materials continues to expand. One of LEED's major accomplishments—saving energy by making buildings more airtight—has had the paradoxical effect of more effectively trapping the gases emitted by the unprecedented number of chemicals used in today's building materials and furnishings. Yet, as the threat from indoor air pollution grows, LEED puts almost no weight on human health factors in deciding whether a building meets its environmental and social goals.

I was lead author of a report on this issue that was released in May [2010], and I recently met with Green Building Council executives, who made it clear that LEED's management is deeply committed to an energy efficient future. Yet it also was apparent that the certification system is unlikely to soon focus on health with respect to hazardous chemicals.

At this point, LEED, a voluntary set of standards created by architects, engineers and builders, can award its highest level of certification—platinum—to a structure that earns no credits for air quality. In practice, the average LEED-certified building achieves only 6 percent of its total points for "indoor environmental quality," the category most closely tied to health, although some of these credits are often given for lighting and thermal comfort rather than assurance of reduced exposure to dangerous substances.

This fact points up a serious flaw in the program: The job of setting standards for new construction—particularly health standards—should not be left to a private-sector organization dominated by members who profit from the sale of goods and services to the building sector.

The potential threats to human health—data suggest that increased chemical exposure in indoor environments may be one reason behind a rapid rise in childhood asthma, for example—require more aggressive action, primarily from the federal government. Because the public interest in healthy, energy-efficient, and environmentally safe buildings is enormous—and well beyond the capacity, financial interests, and willingness of the building industry to manage—the nation needs a comprehensive federal law to control the chemical content of the built environment. LEED is simply not up to the job.

Toxics in Buildings

In 1999, the U.S. Centers for Disease Control and Prevention (CDC) began testing human tissue samples to detect the presence of environmental contaminants. CDC scientists reported that most individuals carry a mixture of metals, plastic polymers, pesticides, solvents, fire retardants, and waterproofing agents, all commonly present in modern buildings. Children often carry higher concentrations than adults.

Many of the chemical ingredients in these building materials are well known to be hazardous to human health. Some are respiratory stressors, neurotoxins, hormone mimics, carcinogens, reproductive hazards, or developmental toxins. Thousands of synthetic and natural chemicals make up modern buildings, and many materials and products "off-gas" and can be inhaled by occupants. Others may erode from metal or plastic water pipes and end up in a glass of water.

The widespread use of such chemicals comes at a time when Americans spend, on average, 90 percent of their time indoors or in vehicles. American children—who increasingly forsake outdoor recreation to occupy themselves for more than seven hours a day with electronic media—spend an astonishing 97 percent of their lives indoors or in cars, according to a recent survey.

In December 2009, the U.S. Environmental Protection Agency (EPA) released a list of chemicals that "may present an unreasonable risk of injury to health and the environment." The EPA list includes four classes of chemicals widely used in the building industry and approved for use by the LEED rating system. These chemicals include phthalates (used as softeners in flexible vinyl products, such as floor and wall coverings); short-chain chlorinated paraffins (used in plastics); PBDEs (used as flame retardants in textiles, plastics, and wire insulation); and perfluorinated chemicals, including PFOA (used for non-stick cookware and stain-resistant materials). Many LEED-certified buildings have been constructed using some of these compounds.

Plastics pose a special problem, as they now comprise nearly 70 percent of the synthetic chemical industry in the United States. More than 100 billion pounds of resins are produced each year, forming many different building materials, including window and door casings, furnishings, electrical wiring, piping, insulation, water and waste conduits, floor coverings, paints, appliances, countertops, lighting fixtures, and electronics.

Hazardous chemicals have become components of LEED-certified indoor environments primarily due to the failures of the federal Toxic Substances Control Act (TSCA) and EPA's neglect of the problem. Congress has given the EPA limited authority to require testing of likely hazardous chemicals in building products. Among nearly 80,000 chemicals in commerce, EPA has required toxicity testing of only 200 in nearly 25 years. These test results led EPA to ban or phase out only five chemicals. The overwhelming majority of chemicals in buildings remain untested, meaning that new products may incorporate tens of thousands of untested chemicals with no government oversight. Since TSCA places the burden of proof of hazard on EPA, nearly all chemicals in building materials have escaped federal testing and regulation.

Regulations in the Building Sector

Many sectors of the economy, including pharmaceuticals and pesticides, are highly regulated by the federal government to protect public health. But the building sector—which now produces $1.25 trillion in annual revenues, roughly 9 percent of U.S. gross domestic product in 2009—has escaped such federal control. The lack of government regulation is explained, in part, by the building industry's enormous financial power, but also by its recent success in creating green building and development standards that give the impression of environmental responsibility and protection of human health.

In fact, programs such as LEED place relatively little emphasis on indoor air quality and the impact of "off-gassing" of chemicals on the health of a building's occupants.

The impetus for the creation of the LEED program was the acknowledgment that more than 100 million buildings in the U.S. consume 76 percent of the nation's electricity. The

U.S. Green Building Council—a private organization with nearly 19,000 members, including developers, engineers, architects, and building materials manufacturers—understandably created LEED to focus primarily on energy conservation.

The LEED scoring system is weighted heavily toward energy conservation. The largest category of possible credits for new construction encourages energy conservation, either directly via use of renewable technologies—solar panels, geothermal wells, insulation—or indirectly through demonstrations of reduced water use, proximity to public transit, or use of locally produced materials.

LEED staff evaluate building performance, assign scores (a total of 100 points is possible), and issue certificates based upon the total award to determine whether "platinum," "gold," or "silver" standards have been achieved. These designations often create eligibility for income tax credits, property tax reductions, and lower interest loans. And these public subsidies often enhance property value.

LEED has no requirement for post-occupancy air quality monitoring for particulate matter or volatile organic compounds. These are primary threats to health, especially among those with background respiratory and cardiovascular disease.

The effect of many energy-conserving design features and materials is to encourage better sealed and insulated buildings. Tighter structures lower the exchange between indoor and outdoor air unless ventilation is carefully monitored and managed. Since indoor air is often more contaminated by synthetic chemicals than outdoor air, the effect may intensify occupants' chemical exposures, increasing health risks.

Creating a Healthy Building Policy

Recently, I worked closely with colleagues at Environment and Human Health Inc., a nonprofit organization comprised of medical doctors, as well as public health and policy experts, to examine these questions. Our report, "LEED Certification:

Where Energy Efficiency Collides with Human Health," called for a federal law to control the chemical content of the built environment. Its purpose should be to protect human health and environmental quality, to encourage materials recycling, and to reduce waste.

What would key elements of a national healthy building policy include?

New chemicals should be tested to understand their threat to human health before they are allowed to be sold. Existing chemicals should also be tested, rather than be exempted, as they are under the Toxic Substances Control Act.

The burden of proof of safety should rest with chemical and building product manufacturers; it's now up to EPA to demonstrate significant danger before the agency may regulate chemicals in commerce. The testing itself should be conducted by an independent, government-supervised institute, but paid for by the manufacturers.

A clear environmental safety standard should also be adopted to prevent further development and sale of persistent and bioaccumulating compounds. Priority should be given to test and eliminate those compounds found in human tissues by the Centers for Disease Control and Prevention.

The chemical contents of building materials and their country of origin should be identified. Without this knowledge, architects, engineers, and consumers have no hope of avoiding products that could lead to environmental damage or ill-health effects.

EPA should maintain a national registry of the chemical content of building products, furnishings, and cleaning products. The registry should also record and update the chemical testing status and recyclability of a product. The agency should create and maintain a single database that identifies chemical toxicity, level of hazard, common sources of exposure, and an assessment of the adequacy of data used to support these classifications.

The government should categorize building products to identify those that contain hazardous compounds; those that have been tested and found to be safe; and those that have been insufficiently tested making a determination of hazard or safety impossible. This database should be freely available on the Internet.

Distinctive "high performance" environmental health standards should be adopted to guide the construction and renovation of schools and surrounding lands. Although LEED has a separate certification system in place for schools, it suffers from the same limited attention to environmental health.

The federal government should create incentives for companies to research and create new chemicals that meet the health, safety, and environmental standards described above. Funding for "green chemistry" initiatives should be significantly increased and focused on benign substitutes for the most widely used and well-recognized toxic substances.

The federal government should take responsibility for codifying these requirements to protect human health in buildings and communities. EPA is the most logical agency for this assignment given its congressionally mandated purpose to protect human health. The Green Building Council should encourage developers to move beyond minimum federal requirements, though this would require substantial changes in the LEED certification system.

LEED has performed a valuable and significant public service, especially by encouraging designs and technologies that conserve energy. The Green Building Council has become a potent force in shaping the future of the building industry. The program, however, does not offer sufficient protection to human health, nor should it be expected to do so, given its limited legal authority, expertise, and financial capacity. It's time to ensure through federal law that green buildings become healthy buildings.

Periodical and Internet Sources Bibliography

The following articles have been selected to supplement the diverse views presented in this chapter.

Vince Catalli and Ralf Nielsen
"The Economics of Sustainable Buildings," *SABMag*, October 6, 2010.

Richard Conniff
"Reconnecting with Nature Through Green Architecture," *Yale Environment 360*, September 3, 2009.

Andy Engel
"Green Building Basics," *Tools of the Trade*, September 18, 2006.

Douglas Fischer
"Do Green Building Standards Minimize Human Health Concerns?," *Scientific American*, June 7, 2010.

Christopher Hawthorne
"Building Better: Emerald Cities," *Sierra*, January/February 2009.

Ben Ikenson
"Liability in the Air," *Builder News*, November 4, 2010.

Vince McLeod and Glenn R. Ketcham
"Take the LEED®: Prevent Indoor Air Quality Issues After New Construction or Renovations," *ALN*, March 1, 2009.

Tracy Schelmetic
"Can a Building Be Both Green and Sick?," ThomasNet News, March 9, 2011. http://news.thomasnet.com.

Jan Ellen Spiegel
"The House That Green Built," *New York Times*, April 20, 2008.

OPPOSING
VIEWPOINTS®
SERIES

CHAPTER 2

How Does Eco-Architecture Impact the Environment?

Chapter Preface

"Sustainable architecture can help put into practice and even encourage a sustainable way of life," states Paola Sassi, an architect and instructor in design and sustainability at the Welsh School of Architecture at Cardiff University. "Not to build for maximum energy, water, materials, and waste efficiency is to place an unacceptable burden on future generations," Sassi continues. In particular, she maintains that rising population growth and living standards will require more natural resources, worsen pollution, and increase humanity's toll on the environment.

Therefore, Sassi believes that architects have pragmatic and moral imperatives to build green. "Sustainable technologies are available, sustainable design strategies have been implemented, and studies have proved that these approaches can contribute positively to reducing the ecological footprint of a society," she asserts. "There aren't any practical or ethical reasons for not designing and building sustainable buildings."

Nonetheless, green designers like Sassi have their detractors. Garry Stevens, former professor of architecture and design science at the University of Sydney, argues that they are out of touch. "Frankly, we suspect that most of these architectural proponents of sustainable design have only the vaguest idea of the realities of their chosen fetish," he contends. Stevens, for instance, complains that glass-covered buildings do not always effectively reduce radiant heat and cause glare.

Moreover, Stevens proposes that sustainable architecture is "a theory tackling a problem that does not need to be tackled" and ignores the true causes of climate change and the energy crisis. "There are many better targets, and none more so than transportation," he claims. "If the architects so passionately advocating sustainable design really wished to contribute to

the cause they profess to espouse, they would not drive a car."
In the following chapter, the authors deliberate the sustainability of eco-architecture.

"*Green building, on average, currently reduces energy use by 30 percent, carbon emissions by 35 percent, and water use by 30 to 50 percent.*"

Eco-Architecture Benefits the Environment

Secretariat of the Commission for Environmental Cooperation (CEC)

The Commission for Environmental Cooperation (CEC) is an international organization established by the United States, Canada, and Mexico to administer the North American Agreement on Environmental Cooperation. In the following viewpoint, the CEC contends that eco-architecture can limit the ecological impacts of buildings throughout construction, use, and demolition. Green building can address climate change and emissions by reducing the energy consumed for lighting, heating, and cooling, it states, and reusable and recyclable components and better product designs can cut construction waste and the use of raw materials. The CEC concludes that numerous organizations and nations are aggressively pursuing several initiatives, such as calling for zero net-energy and carbon-neutral buildings for the future.

Secretariat of the Commission for Environmental Cooperation (CEC), "Green Building in North America: Opportunities and Challenges," Commission for Environmental Cooperation, 2008, pp. 16–18, 22–24, 26, 28–30, 34, 36–37. Copyright © Commission for Environmental Cooperation, 2008. Reproduced by permission.

As you read, consider the following questions:

1. What are the consequences of poor patterns of building development, as claimed by the CEC?

2. What are the energy reductions for advanced green buildings, according to the CEC?

3. As described in the viewpoint, what does the Swedish study on energy-efficiency measures indicate?

Environmental impacts of buildings occur throughout all life stages of a building—site selection, design, location, construction, use, renovation, and demolition. Building decisions made throughout these life stages also affect business value, worker health and productivity, and social or "quality of life" issues.

Direct environmental impacts that result from the construction and operation of buildings include greenhouse gases and other air emissions related to energy use, water use and discharge, storm water runoff, impacts related to building materials, solid waste from various stages of a building's life, and indoor air quality. Secondary impacts are generally associated with building product life cycles, infrastructure development, and transportation systems.

Data collected from Canada, Mexico and the United States illustrate these impacts.

In Canada, buildings are responsible for:

- 33 percent of all energy used;

- 50 percent of natural resources consumed;

- 12 percent of nonindustrial water used;

- 25 percent of landfill waste generated;

- 10 percent of airborne particulates produced; and

- 35 percent of greenhouse gases emitted.

In Mexico, buildings are responsible for:

• 17 percent of all energy used;

• 25 percent of all electricity used;

• 20 percent of all carbon dioxide emissions;

• 5 percent of potable water consumption; and

• 20 percent of the waste generated.

In the United States, buildings account for:

• 40 percent of total energy use;

• 12 percent of total water consumption;

• 68 percent of total electricity consumption;

• 38 percent of total carbon dioxide emissions; and

• 60 percent of total nonindustrial waste generation.

The impact is especially profound in terms of greenhouse gas emissions. Every year, buildings in North America cause more than 2,200 MT [megatons] of CO_2 to be released into the atmosphere, about 35 percent of the continent's total. Hundreds of coal-fired power plants, a key source of greenhouse gas emissions, are currently on the drawing boards in the United States. According to one report, 76 percent of the energy produced by these plants will go to operate buildings.

Beyond individual buildings, poor patterns of building development often lead to congestion and inefficient use of land, resulting in greater energy consumption and travel time, loss of productivity, polluted runoff to surface water and wastewater treatment systems, loss of agricultural lands, fragmented habitats, and fiscal stress to local communities. Two case studies from Toronto indicate that residents of sprawling neighborhoods tend to emit more greenhouse gases per person and suffer more traffic fatalities.

Urban water runoff is another important building-related impact. Buildings, and transportation infrastructure that serve them, replace natural surfaces with impermeable materials, typically creating runoff that washes pollutants and sediments into surface water. Urban runoff is the fourth-leading cause of impairment of rivers, third-leading for lakes, and second for estuaries in the United States, and a significant problem in many parts of Mexico and Canada as well. In Mexico City, most rainwater flows on impermeable surfaces to the city drainage system; only a small proportion (11 percent) is re-charged into the aquifer, causing a greater dependence on neighboring basins and increasing the risk of flooding.

Benefits of Green Building

The benefits of green building are well documented. The US-GBC [US Green Building Council] estimates that green build-ing, on average, currently reduces energy use by 30 percent, carbon emissions by 35 percent, and water use by 30 to 50 percent, and generates waste cost savings of 50 to 90 percent. In addition, green building can help foster stronger communi-ties and provide important benefits to human health and productivity. . . .

SAVING ENERGY

Green building addresses climate change and other energy-related air emissions in two basic ways: first (and most importantly), by reducing the amount of energy used to light, heat, cool and operate buildings and their appliances, and sec-ond, by substituting for what currently is mostly carbon-based energy with alternatives that do not involve the production of greenhouse gases and other harmful air emissions. It is com-mon now for more advanced green buildings to routinely re-duce energy usage by 30, 40, or even 50 percent over conven-tional buildings, with the most efficient buildings now performing more than 70 percent better than conventional properties.

IMPROVING WATER USAGE

Green building uses a number of techniques to improve water quality and availability. These techniques can help reduce water usage, provide for on-site cleaning and reuse of wastewater, and on-site filtering of storm water. Water management is a significant cost and an important environmental issue in all three countries. Water stress is particularly high in parts of Mexico, the United States, and western Canada.

REDUCING WASTE

Reducing waste through better product design, recycling, and re-use of materials will result in tremendous reductions in both raw material usage and also in associated environmental impacts, as well as the cost to the private sector and local governments of disposing of these materials. Building-related construction and demolition debris totals approximately 136 million tons per year in the United States, accounting for nearly 60 percent of the total nonindustrial waste generation there. An estimated 20 to 30 percent of building-related construction and demolition debris is recovered for processing and recycling. In Canada, construction, renovation, and demolition waste accounts for about 17 to 21 percent of the total mass of waste landfilled annually. The volume of demolition waste in Mexico City is estimated between 3,500 and 5,000 tons a day. Reducing construction waste and creating reusable and recyclable building components are key strategies in addressing these environmental impacts.

BUILDING STRONG COMMUNITIES

Green building is a key component to building healthy, vibrant, and economically strong communities. Leading communities throughout the world recognize that people want to live in places with a strong sense of community, attractive and comfortable homes, walkable streets, and plentiful green spaces, and proximity to transit, shops, and work.

IMPROVING HUMAN HEALTH AND PRODUCTIVITY

While energy-related issues drive much of the green building policy discussion, for many businesses, energy costs represent a marginal cost of doing business as compared with the salaries of employees. Substantial research supports the benefits to human health and productivity from green features such as daylighting, increased natural air ventilation, and moisture reduction, and the use of low-emitting floor carpets, glues, paint and other interior finishes and furnishings.

Poor indoor air quality exacerbates asthma, allergies, and the spread of influenza, and is the cause of sick building syndrome and contributes to Legionnaires' disease. In the United States, the annual cost of building-related sickness is estimated to be $58 billion. According to researchers, green building has the potential to generate an additional $200 billion annually in worker performance in the United States by creating offices with better indoor air.

Green Building and Greenhouse Gas Emissions

Reports from leading scientists throughout the world underline the need for urgent global action on climate change. The IPCC [Intergovernmental Panel on Climate Change] projects that without more immediate action to limit greenhouse gas emissions, global warming could cause irreversible and possibly catastrophic consequences.

Three recent reports illustrate that energy-efficient buildings are one of the quickest and cheapest ways to reduce significantly greenhouse gas emissions.

MITIGATING CLIMATE CHANGE WITH NET ECONOMIC BENEFIT

According to a recent IPCC report, buildings represent the greatest opportunity for considerable reductions in CO_2 emissions. Its fourth assessment report states that about 30 percent of the projected global greenhouse gas emissions in the building sector can be avoided by 2030 with net economic benefit.

Architecture 2030 Challenge Targets

Hundreds of architecture firms and other individuals have adopted the Architecture 2030 Challenge, which calls for the global architecture and building community to adopt the following targets:

- All new buildings, developments and major renovations shall be designed to meet a fossil fuel, greenhouse gas–emitting, energy-consumption performance standard of 50 per cent of the regional (or country) average for that building type.

- At a minimum, an equal amount of existing building area shall be renovated annually to meet a fossil fuel, greenhouse gas–emitting, energy-consumption performance standard of 50 per cent of the regional (or country) average for that building type.

- The fossil fuel reduction standard for all new buildings shall be increased to 60 per cent in 2010, 70 per cent in 2015, 80 per cent in 2020, 90 per cent in 2025 and carbon neutral in 2030 (using no fossil fuel, greenhouse gas–emitting energy to operate). These targets may be accomplished by implementing innovative sustainable design strategies, generating on-site renewable power, and/or purchasing (20 per cent maximum) renewable energy and/or certified renewable energy credits.

Peter Droege,
100% Renewable: Energy Autonomy in Action,
Sterling, VA: Earthscan, 2009.

According to the report, limiting CO_2 emissions would also improve indoor and outdoor air quality, improve social welfare, and enhance energy security.

CURBING GLOBAL ENERGY DEMAND GROWTH

A recent study by the international consulting firm Mc-Kinsey & Company indicates that building energy-efficiency measures are some of the cheapest and most cost-effective ways to reduce carbon emissions worldwide. It also notes that these measures would require no reduction in quality of life or comfort.

THE COSTS OF CUTTING CARBON IN DIFFERENT WAYS

A study by a Swedish power utility finds that energy-efficiency measures, such as improving insulation and water heaters and switching to low-energy lighting systems, can save money and cut tremendous amounts of greenhouse gas emissions. Insulation improvements alone could save more than 1.7 gigatonnes of CO_2 by 2030, lighting improvement could eliminate close to 0.4 gigatonnes, and water heating improvements of about 0.5 gigatonnes. According to the study, the investment costs to achieve these savings would be more than compensated for by a decrease in the costs for the energy.

Calling for Aggressive Improvement in North America

An increasing number of organizations and institutions in North America are calling for aggressive energy performance improvements in the building sector. A number of important efforts are looking at ways to achieve widespread adoption of carbon-neutral and net zero-energy buildings in North America.

AIA 2030 CHALLENGE

In 2005, the American Institute of Architects (AIA) issued the 2030 Challenge, which sets forth a target and schedule to be achieved by carbon-neutral buildings by 2030. The Royal Architectural Institute of Canada (RAIC), the US [Conference] of Mayors, and the International Council for Local Environmental Initiatives (ICLEI) have joined this initiative. In addition, over 650 US cities have adopted it. In 2007, the AIA, the American Society of Heating, Refrigerating and Air-Conditioning Engineers (ASHRAE), Architecture 2030, the Illuminating Engineering Society of North America (IES), and the US Green Building Council, supported by the United States Department of Energy, signed a memorandum of understanding focusing on designing net zero-energy buildings, with a final goal of carbon-neutral buildings by 2030.

WBCSD

The World Business Council for Sustainable Development (WBCSD) began working in 2006 toward developing a path to net zero-energy buildings by 2050. The WBCSD effort is initially targeting China, India, Brazil, the United States and the European Union for creation of these buildings. The core group of companies supporting this effort includes United Technologies [Corporation], LaFarge, CEMEX, Kansal [Group], EDF, Philips, DuPont, Gaz de France, Sonae Sierra and Tokyo Electric Power Company.

OTHER CALLS FOR AGGRESSIVE IMPROVEMENTS

In 2006, the Canadian government launched the first phase of a net zero-energy housing initiative. This initial phase is part of a five-year, community-scale demonstration aimed at completing 1,500 net zero-energy homes across Canada by 2011. The Living Building Challenge, operated by the USGBC's Cascadia chapter, requires a number of performance benchmarks, including the requirement that 100 percent of the building's energy needs must be supplied by on-site renewable energy on a net annual basis.

The United States Department of Energy's Building America program conducts research in partnership with the private sector to produce homes on a community scale that consume on average 30 to 90 percent less energy than conventional homes, with the goal of developing by 2020 zero energy homes (ZEH) that produce more on-site renewable energy than they consume from the grid. The California Solar Initiative, launched in 2007, aims for installation of 3,000 megawatts of new, solar-produced electricity at one million new and existing residential and commercial buildings by 2017.

> *"In reality, the greenest thing you can do is to continue the life of an existing building."*

Eco-Architecture Does Not Benefit the Environment

Jane Powell

Jane Powell is a renovator of old homes and the author of archi-tectural design books that specialize in bungalows. In the follow-ing viewpoint, she claims that sustainable building practices and developments threaten the environment and the nation's neigh-borhoods. Powell maintains that green developers consume enor-mous resources, demolish sturdy historic homes, and discard valuable materials to build cheap, faddish construction projects that will not last. The rapid growth of the population and cities do not justify more building, Powell insists, even if it is green building. Instead, she advocates the conservation of old build-ings—not just "trophy" ones—through maintenance or rehabili-tation.

As you read, consider the following questions:

1. What are green developers' arguments for the destruc-tion of historic buildings, as told by Powell?

Jane Powell, "Smart Growth, Green Building, and Other Oxymorons," *American Bunga-low*, no. 62, May–August 2009, pp. 100–103. Copyright © 2009 American Bungalow Magazine. Reproduced by permission.

2. How does Powell compare the sustainability of green buildings to old buildings?

3. In the author's opinion, how must attitudes change about old, historic buildings?

Love the word "oxymoron" because it has "moron" right there in the word. It comes from the Greek, and it refers to a pair of words that contradict each other, or cancel each other out, like "pointed (i.e., smart) foolishness," "original copy," or "lead balloon."

Or "smart growth" and "green building."

Today there is a lot of pointed foolishness going around, particularly in regard to land use and historic buildings. Take "smart growth." Who, after all, would be in favor of dumb growth? Smart growth, as planning consultant Eben Fodor has remarked, is merely the "planned, orderly destruction of the remaining natural environment." Perhaps, as [CNN and TBS founder] Ted Turner suggested, we should call it "less-stupid growth." In my view, it will soon rest on the same trash heap as "urban renewal," "festival marketplace," "pedestrian mall" and all the other planning fads of the last 40 years. Yet every developer can spout the smart-growth party line about how the huge development he is proposing for your single-family neighborhood (which will be called La Boheme or Allegro or something suitably "urban") will prevent farmland being paved over elsewhere, at the same time that his company is paving over said farmland and calling it "Cottonwood Creek" after the trees that were destroyed to make room for the 4,000-square-foot homes he's building there on quarter-acre lots.

Then there's "green building." In addition to the "smart growth" argument that goes along with these new blights on the landscape, there's the canard ("fabricated report," "groundless rumor") that the new buildings that are replacing old historic ones will be "green." Explain to me exactly what is green about tearing down buildings that were built with hundreds of board feet of old-growth timber, which have lasted 80 to

100 years or more, in order to throw up obscenely dense buildings with cheap metal windows, crappy second-growth lumber and fake stucco, even if they do have solar panels? In reality, the greenest thing you can do is to continue the life of an existing building—ideally by maintaining it, but if it's too late for that, then by restoring or rehabilitating it.

Discarding the Historic, Already-Built Environment

Often developers argue that they are going to salvage and re-cycle the old building materials—and well they may. But I can guarantee there's one thing that will not get reused: lath. I'm about as obsessive as they come, and even I don't reuse lath. And yet lath, like everything else in an old building, is made from old-growth timber. And it is nothing short of criminal to send that wood, which took thousands of years to grow, splintered and useless to a landfill.

"Infill" is another buzzword that's often seen as being part of "smart growth." One would think that infill meant building on vacant lots, or maybe building a little cottage behind a house or a rental unit over a garage. But in practice it means tearing down an existing small building in order to (and I use the term deliberately) throw up a much larger one. Almost always it's a historic building that is destroyed—possibly one that was abandoned, or neglected, or simply had the fault of being small and not architecturally distinguished. Those who had it destroyed argued that (a) it would have cost too much to fix it or (b) saving it wasn't worth sacrificing the greater good of "density near transit." Doing either would have meant the project wouldn't "pencil out"—that is, generate the bloated profit to which they feel entitled.

Conserve, Not Build Our Way Out

Nationwide, 577 historic houses are demolished every day. During the 1990s, 722,000 pre-1920s houses were demolished. Many were bungalows. In every city, historic buildings are being sacrificed for some perceived short-term gain, and we can't ever get those buildings back.

On its website, the Association of Bay Area Governments has this definition of smart growth: "Revitalizing the already-built environment." I'm for that. But in practice, the already-built environment is often discarded, to be replaced by faceless buildings with an average life span of 30 or 40 years. And yet there are those who insist this is progress, although as [journalist] Russell Baker said, "Usually, terrible things that are done with the excuse that progress requires them are not progress at all, but just terrible things."

There has been a lot of talk about the New Urbanism in recent years, but not much about the Old Urbanism. Most cities already have what the New Urbanists call "transit-oriented developments." They were called streetcar suburbs, at least until somebody stupidly ripped out the streetcars. Now, it's true that those bungalow suburbs were built at the expense of old-growth forests and other nonrenewable resources, and it's even true that a bungalow is not the most efficient use of a building footprint. (The most efficient use of a building footprint for a single-family home is a foursquare, so all you foursquare owners can congratulate yourselves.) The point is that a lot of the old urbanism could have been—and can still be—reused.

The population of the U.S. has passed 300 million, a 50 percent increase since 1967 and a doubling of the population in our lifetimes. We have already exceeded the carrying capacity of our finite planet, but apparently the great majority of people still believe that somehow we can build our way out of that reality. Melissa [Holbrook] Pierson, author of *The Place You Love Is Gone*, wrote: "It is real, that choking breathlessness you feel, as if on an overcrowded elevator that is momentarily stuck. It is real, that childish despair on watching the things that made up a pleasant universe loaded onto a flatbed truck and getting smaller and smaller as it disappears down the highway. It is real, the acceleration of loss."

Until now, most of us humans have lived off this planet on the assumption that "there's plenty more where that came from." But like Captain Kirk [in the television series *Star Trek*], when Scotty says, "I canna give ye no more power, Cap'n!" we still figure Scotty will pull some miraculous stunt that will save us. In reality, we cannot build our way out of the pickle we've put ourselves in. We have to conserve our way out of it. According to the Environmental Protection Agency, 48 percent of U.S. greenhouse gas emissions are produced by the construction and operation of buildings. Even a new green building made with sustainable materials still uses up resources and energy, and it will be 40 years or more before the energy it saves by being operated under green principles balances out the energy that was used to build it. By contrast, an existing building has embodied energy; all the energy that was used in its construction is already sequestered. To put it another way, that energy is safely in a bank that is insured against failure if properly protected and cared for.

Even the National Trust for Historic Preservation, which had jumped unquestioningly onto the smart growth bandwagon several years ago, is now promoting the sustainability of historic buildings, saying it makes no sense to recycle plastic, newsprint, bottles and cans while throwing away entire buildings, and they are trying to refute the misconceptions about energy efficiency and older buildings—a difficult task, given the huge advertising budgets of new-home builders and window manufacturers.

Changing the Consciousness About Historic Buildings

Still, there are many people who profit from growth, and they beat that drum so loudly it's hard to be heard over it. A professor at the University of Colorado, Al Bartlett, had this to say:

"We in the United States are in a culture that worships growth. Steady growth of populations of our towns and cities is the goal toward which the powerful promotional groups in our communities continuously aspire. If a town's population is growing, the town is said to be 'healthy,' or 'vibrant,' and if the population is not growing the town is said to be 'stagnant.' Something that is not growing should properly be called 'stable.' Yet, the promoters of growth universally use the word 'stagnant' to describe the condition of stability, because 'stagnant' suggests something unpleasant."

So now that I've caused you to lapse into total and utter despair, perhaps you are asking, "Is there any hope? Is there anything we can do?" Well, yes and no. We need desperately to change the consciousness in this country so that old buildings are valued—not just the trophy buildings, often referred to as "the mansions of the rich, dead white guys," but *all* old buildings. I would like to see a time where it will simply be unthinkable to destroy a historic building. Think that's impossible? Consider this: In the 1960s smoking was common and socially acceptable—smoking at work, in movie theaters, grocery stores, restaurants, cars, planes, in front of children, etc. Now, there is almost nowhere it's permissible, and it's no longer socially acceptable—smokers are huddled outside, and non-smokers feel free to complain about secondhand smoke.

I believe that same change of consciousness is possible in regard to historic buildings. But it will require that people (such as yourselves) begin to question the dominant paradigm. Unfortunately, for that to happen you will have to get up out of your comfy Morris chair and actually DO something. It isn't enough to merely belong to your neighborhood association, or send membership money every year to your local historic preservation organization. You need to show up at meetings, write letters, educate your neighbors, write about it on your blog, run for office, and all that other tedious grassroots stuff that is required in order to change things. The original arts and crafts movement proponents were politically and socially active, and they truly believed that living in these houses, and having well-designed objects, would make people better citizens. It's time for us to prove them right.

"This net-zero house is about more than generating surplus energy. It's about offering a model for a new way of building—and living."

Large Houses Can Be Eco-Friendly

Blair Kamin

In the following viewpoint, Blair Kamin claims that a green 2,675-square-foot house in Chicago, Illinois, achieves net-zero status, or produces as much energy as it consumes. Kamin explains that the house's cleverly designed roof hides solar panels that generate 40 percent above its projected annual energy use and collects rainwater. Also, the house's layout, use of recycled and sustainable materials, geothermal heating and cooling machines, and gray water system demonstrate that eco-architecture and design will innovate how homes are built, he maintains. Kamin, who won the Pulitzer Prize for criticism in 1999, is the architecture critic for the Chicago Tribune.

As you read, consider the following questions:

1. Why are there only about one hundred net-zero homes in the country, in Kamin's view?

2. How does Michael Yannell's house maximize the use of windows and sunlight, as described by the author?

3. How does Yannell's house's gray water system conserve water, as told by Kamin?

Michael Yannell's ComEd bill is almost surely less than yours.

Yannell, 44, lives in a new Chicago home that is designed to be net-zero energy, which means it will produce as much energy as it consumes—or more. The $1.6 million, 2,675-square-foot house is the first of its kind in Chicago, which has achieved green sheen with its energy-saving public buildings and scores of planted roofs.

Yet the Yannell House, which has four bedrooms, two bathrooms and three occupants (the owner and his two cats), is more than a mere technical feat. Clean-lined outside and light-filled within, it issues an elegant rebuttal to the super-size, decoration-slathered McMansions that exemplify the pre-crash age of excess.

"I wanted to make a big, splashy statement to the city that that was the wrong direction," said Yannell, standing next to a kitchen countertop partly made of recycled newspapers. He's lived in the house since April [2009].

A Statement House

A pharmacist at Rush University Medical Center, he is the ideal client for this sort of thing, possessing both ample funds and a zealous level of commitment. By his own calculation, he spent 40 hours researching energy-saving appliances. At first, he simply wanted to build an energy-efficient house. He went to Farr Associates, one of the city's top green firms. When the architects introduced him to the more ambitious net-zero concept, he said "yes" to the upgrade.

"We thought this was a gift from God," Jonathan Boyer, a Farr principal and the house's chief designer, said with a laugh.

If nothing else, the house should shatter stereotypes, proving that hyper-green construction is as possible in frequently cloudy Chicago as in sun-drenched Colorado.

"It can be done in pretty much any climate," said Ren Anderson of the National Renewable Energy Laboratory in Golden, Colo.

Yet it costs more here than there and, besides, defining exactly what constitutes net zero can be elusive. It's been said that net-zero houses require net-zero occupants. Forget it if you're going to flood your trees in outdoor lights or stick energy-sucking plasma TVs on walls. Yannell, as you might expect, has two energy-saving LCD TVs.

"They have kill switches, so they draw no power in the off mode," he said.

However they're defined, net-zero houses offer the tantalizing prospect of off-the-grid living, where each house serves as its own power plant.

Though it gets some electricity from ComEd at night, the Yannell House takes a major step down this road. Just don't expect a net-zero revolution any time soon. The house's green features added 10 percent to 15 percent in up-front costs, and it could take years to recoup that premium, Boyer said. That helps explain why there are only about 100 net-zero houses scattered around the U.S.

Still, the Yannell House is a statement house, not a model for mass production, and the statement it makes along the Metra tracks at 4895 N. Ravenswood Ave. is exactly right: A well-designed net-zero house should be about more than slapping a huge array of photovoltaic panels on a roof.

The design begins with Boyer's well-conceived floor plan—a U shape that consists of two non-identical wings joined by a foyer. This arrangement nicely breaks down the house's mass. It looks like two houses, not a small museum, as some big modern houses do these days.

Each wing has broad bands of triple-paned windows facing southward, drawing in lots of natural light, except when the roof's carefully calculated overhangs block the high summer sun. The south wing, which houses the kitchen as well as living and dining areas, is about 10 feet shorter than the north wing, home to bedrooms, an office and a music room. That's so light can filter into the second-story bedrooms and their views aren't blocked.

Environmental Expressionism

The house is equally good at projecting its identity outward.

Its exuberant "butterfly" roof folds upward with sculptural verve, even as it cleverly hides the house's 48 photovoltaic panels and doubles as a rainwater collector. Coming closer, you encounter a delicate "rain screen" facade, consisting of an outer layer of warm cedar panels and cool, fiber-cement board panels. An inner layer provides thermal insulation. The rain screen seems to breath like a skin.

"Environmental expressionism," Boyer calls it.

The interior is remarkably light-filled and airy, fully taking advantage of the house's unencumbered views to the south.

In the expansive south wing, the underside of the butterfly roof seems to alight on a long steel beam that allows the combined kitchen-living-dining area to be column-free. Yet the beam comes down low enough to give the expansive room a sense of intimacy. That impression is furthered by the presence of such tactile details as wall tiles made of recycled green-glass bottles.

Only the passing Metra trains interrupt the serenity, and their sound is muffled by the triple-paned glass.

The north wing offers pleasures of its own: views back across the courtyard, plus a master bedroom and guest bedroom that feel like tree houses.

While construction joints are expressed, in keeping with Chicago's architectural tradition, many of the house's energy-saving features are concealed.

In the basement, you find geothermal heating and cooling machines linked to three wells dug 250 feet down. Also in the basement are multiple filters for the house's gray water system, which converts spent water from the house's washing machine to clean water that can be used in its toilets. It's believed to be the first gray water system in a Chicago single-family home.

Boyer projects that the array of photovoltaic and solar-thermal panels will generate 18,000 kilowatt-hours a year, exceeding the house's projected energy use by 40 percent.

"So far, we're doing great," he said, but he's cautious because it's summer and there's been plenty of sunshine.

To date, Yannell had paid one ComEd bill of $29.57, despite feeding his surplus energy into the grid.

"ComEd hasn't set up my meter to credit me," he said. Even when it does, he expects to pay a basic monthly fee of about $20.

Future finances aside, the most important lesson of the Yannell House is clear: This net-zero house is about more than generating surplus energy. It's about offering a model for a new way of building—and living.

"It is simply too easy to rationalize outsized homes and justify their excess by
wrapping them in a loud green ribbon."

Large Houses Cannot Be Eco-Friendly

Jason F. McLennan

*In the following viewpoint, Jason F. McLennan criticizes the
claim that large, green single-family homes can be sustainable.
When it comes to efficiently using resources, size does matter,
and truly sustainable design encompasses not only energy efficiency and the use of green materials, McLennan argues, but
also appropriate square footage per person. Therefore, he urges
prospective homeowners to choose quality in construction over
quantity in space to set maximum house sizes and square footage allowances based on the number of occupants. McLennan is
chief executive officer of the Cascadia region Green Building
Council and author of* The Philosophy of Sustainable Design.

As you read, consider the following questions:

1. According to the author, "green mansions" are symptomatic of what larger problems?

Jason F. McLennan, "The Righteous Small House: Challenging House Size and the Irre-
sponsible American Dream," *Trim Tab*, First Quarter, 2009, pp. 17–21. Reproduced by
permission.

2. What statistics does McLennan provide to support his argument that resources are used inefficiently to build homes and home sizes are disproportionate?

3. What recommendations does the author offer for square footage per person?

A house must be built on solid foundations if it is to last. The same principle applies to man, otherwise he too will sink back into the soft ground and become swallowed up by the world of illusion.

—*Sai Baba*

I recently toured a residential subdivision whose grandiose homes were aggressively promoted as green. The developer and builder used a rating system to quantify the extent to which they had built sustainability into each structure. I was drawn to the project because of its claims of responsibility; I was repelled by it when I observed its inherent hypocrisy.

How, under any circumstances, can a 6,000-square-foot single-family home be considered green? Something is terribly wrong with a system that ranks such a dwelling high on the green scale when it is intended to house only two to five people. Such oversized homes—with their three-car garages, bonus rooms, great rooms, etc.—are nothing less than mini-mansions ("starter castles," as I call them) and have no business being associated with green building, even when they incorporate green features.

In my opinion, the existence of oxymoronic "green mansions" is symptomatic of a larger set of problems. Yes, the design and building communities need to establish universal guidelines to define truly green standards, and communicate the ecological notion that "less is more." But perhaps more importantly, American society must realign its values when it comes to house size. With builders overbuilding, buyers being taught to embrace excess, lenders focusing more on size than value, each link in the chain weakens the one that follows. It is incumbent upon us as leaders in the green movement to educate consumers on how and why to seek saner, greener relationships with their homes.

This [viewpoint] explores two fundamental topics regarding the intersection between lifestyle and sustainability:

1. How big can a home get before it is simply too big to be called green, regardless of its design and materials?

2. From a sustainability standpoint, what size house should we seek? What guidelines should we follow when selecting a home? Should developers take responsibility for limiting the size of homes they build?

At What Point Does Size Cancel Out Sustainability?

Green homes require more than the token placement of solar panels and the use of recycled-content materials. True sustainability must go beyond tangible design and construction and encompass a philosophical commitment to green living.

A larger structure can meet multiple green standards; it can even impose a smaller environmental footprint than smaller homes. But it is simply too easy to rationalize outsized homes and justify their excess by wrapping them in a loud green ribbon.

The industry must follow consistent guidelines and increase public awareness of this growing problem—that is also related to the housing and financial crisis the country is currently in. When all segments of the market work together, green building will evolve from a guilt-removing fashion to a far-reaching instrument of change.

According to the National Association of Home Builders, the average size of a new single-family American residence in 1950 was 983 square feet. Today, it is nearly 2500 square feet. As home sizes ballooned over that time, family size shrank.

The U.S. Census Bureau reports that in 1950, an average American family consisted of 3.8 people; today's average family contains 2.6 people.

These figures prove how inefficiently we use our resources when we build homes with such drastically disproportionate size-to-occupant ratios. Instead, as we go forward, we must adhere to a stricter code of square footage per person, particularly when we speak of green projects.

Plenty of people live in small houses and live what they like to think is an ideal eco-existence. But house size alone does not always relate to responsible resource use. When a childless couple or a one-child family lives in a relatively "small" house but their square-footage-per-person rates are high, they are not living as green as they might think. I am concerned less with total house size and more with relative resource use and quality green design.

I speak to this subject from personal experience as co-head of a blended family with four kids. As our family has grown, my wife and I have lived in homes of varying shapes and sizes—in apartments and single-family homes set in urban centers and rural areas. I've seen what does and doesn't work for family residences, and I've learned that a well-designed home or apartment can be small and functional at the same time.

Through her writing, Sarah Susanka has helped promote the desirability of living Not So Big. She has made the small house cool again, while calling into question what might be missing in the lives of those who settle into such massive physical spaces. Sarah's work celebrates the idea of restraint, which is sorely lacking in our culture. When did our grandparents' notion of "plenty" become "not enough" to 21st-century homeowners, her readers ask? When did the three-car garage, which more often serves as storage for unneeded junk than for vehicles, become a standard feature? When did we decide that we require separate rooms for living, reading, eating and recreation?

The Money Pit

The market-driven interest in size for the sake of size creates a vicious financial and resource-wasting cycle. Buyers spend more on their homes, more to heat and cool them, more to clean them and more to fill them with possessions. Worse yet, most oversized homes are built by cookie-cutter developers who meet the market demand for square footage by compromising on design and material quality. It is amazing how so few large "custom" homes are conceived and built without architects. The results speak for themselves with subdivision after subdivision of poorly designed boxes with terrible site integration, badly designed interior spaces and awkward floor plans. People spend hundreds of thousands of dollars on flimsy dumb boxes with tacked on columns, stainless steel fronted appliances and badly labeled "great rooms" and think somehow they are getting value. The "builder-plan" trend has dumbed down the building profession and resulted in a scarcity of true craftsmanship.

Instead, both sides of the industry (buyers and builders alike) should focus on quality rather than quantity, reinvesting in healthier materials, more durable construction and alternative energy sources in tandem with quality design led by architects and designers. A home should be judged by the quality of its details and craftsmanship rather than the size of its shadow.

Changing the Perception of Value

There are so many things wrong with the model of building massive houses. Consumers usually have a finite amount of money with which to build a home, but societal rules—established, I believe, by developers, builders and lenders in conjunction with societal mores that view "more is better"—dictate that value relates to square footage. The larger the home, the greater the cost ... so if a larger home costs the same as a smaller home, the former is supposedly a better

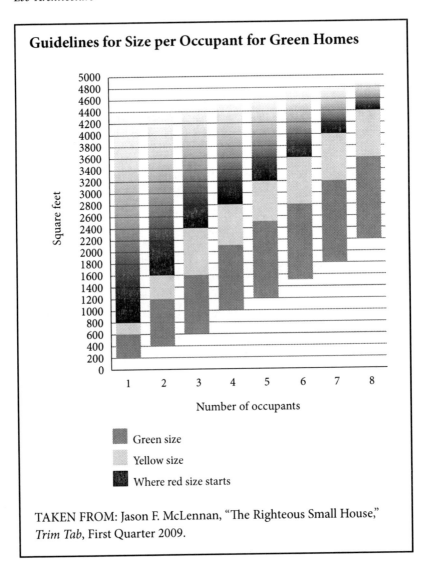

Guidelines for Size per Occupant for Green Homes

Square feet (y-axis): 0, 200, 400, 600, 800, 1000, 1200, 1400, 1600, 1800, 2000, 2200, 2400, 2600, 2800, 3000, 3200, 3400, 3600, 3800, 4000, 4200, 4400, 4600, 4800, 5000

Number of occupants (x-axis): 1, 2, 3, 4, 5, 6, 7, 8

Legend:
- Green size
- Yellow size
- Where red size starts

TAKEN FROM: Jason F. McLennan, "The Righteous Small House," *Trim Tab*, First Quarter 2009.

deal. But it's not, not by a long shot. In order to expand home size and keep costs down, builders cut corners and consumers lose. I've seen many residents who move into giant new houses and can't figure out why they don't feel comfortable inside— and they don't understand that it's the poorly designed spaces. Feng shui does in fact matter. Buyers' joy fades quickly and the reality of living in large, charmless boxes sets in.

A well-built house should far outlive its first owners. And all who dwell there through the years should be allowed to enjoy the comfort that comes with responsibility.

Unfortunately, these misaligned values are rife throughout the system. When buyers seek financing for a given property, lenders look for "comps' in order to establish monetary value. Homes are valued based on a narrow range of shallow attributes, location and size. But the mortgage lending community doesn't factor in design quality or sustainability when it assesses a home; it measures square footage primarily. People seeking to do something durable and innovative see their efforts valued less than if they simply built what everyone else was building—surely a perverse incentive if there ever was one. Not surprisingly, smaller homes are particularly undervalued and even though it is more likely that someone with lower energy bills and operating costs can afford to pay their mortgages—they are penalized.

The Green Square Foot Metric

If the industry embraced a national square-footage-per-resident standard, then designers, builders, buyers and lenders could quantify a home's green quotient.

Such a system would provide a concrete method with which to determine whether a house is green or simply green-washed. Smaller, well-built and well-designed houses could become a cornerstone of a new, more responsible lending institution that moved us back from the precipice of the crashing housing market.

First things first: I propose that the design/build community set a maximum house size. Homes exceeding a certain size just wouldn't be built or purchased. Secondly, I recommend that the size-per-person should range from 200 to 800 square feet, depending on the depth of green design for the first three people in a household. When more than three people reside in a house, an additional 400 square feet per person could be used.

This system mandates that no house exceed 4400 square feet—ever. Such a structure is still huge; but using the chart as a guide, it must provide shelter for eight or more people in order to meet sustainability guidelines.

As family size grows, home size does not necessarily have to increase to accommodate human comfort. (For example, you don't add another kitchen or entryway every time a child is born, you simply make them slightly bigger.) Siblings might share bedrooms, family members can share bathrooms, etc. Yes, a separate family room is appealing when multiple kids are involved, and an enclosed garage helps keep the rain off the car. But the greenest solution is what people choose NOT to build.

The Big Bottom Line

1. The average American family house or condominium, which today is built for three people, should be no larger than 1600 square feet in order to be considered green. (This is more than 600 square feet larger than the house of the 1950s but approximately 900 square feet smaller than the average house today.) Houses need to shrink again. This would do a lot to avoid a future housing crisis.

2. If people have more money and are looking for a new place to live, the compelling message should not be to move into a larger home, but rather to invest in quality and design and to downsize or "rightsize" based on your family size.

3. Working at home drastically reduces greenhouse gas emissions as transportation impacts are avoided. Additional square footage can be justified if people are working at home a significant amount of time. In these cases, I would propose a maximum 200 square feet bonus allowance to accommodate telecommuting for each working adult.

4. The square-foot-per-person metric lessens as more people join a household. (Sharing is also green.) So house size shrinks from 600 square feet per person down to 450 square feet per person as an overall average.

As professionals leading the charge toward greener ways of living, we must challenge assumptions that hinder our progress. Responsibility naturally breeds sustainability.

> *"Today, the complaints about sprawl are louder than ever, but as in the past, they are built on an extremely shaky foundation of class-based aesthetic assumptions and misinformation."*

Urban Sprawl Can Be Beneficial

Robert Bruegmann

Robert Bruegmann is a professor in the College of Architecture and the Arts at the University of Illinois at Chicago and author of Sprawl: A Compact History. *In the following viewpoint, he defends urban sprawl, or the expansion of low-density neighborhoods around urban areas. According to him, most assumptions about urban sprawl are incorrect; it is neither accelerating nor the root of increased automobile use, commutes, congestion, and carbon emissions. On the contrary, Bruegmann points out that increasing densities and public transportation will not reduce energy consumption or pollution, and plans to curb urban sprawl have backfired. What is bad is its flawed concept, which distracts from the real and urgent problems for cities, he concludes.*

As you read, consider the following questions:

1. How are cities and suburbs in the United States changing, as purported by the author?

2. As proposed by Bruegmann, what would be possible if everyone in the affluent West spread out to single-family homes in low-density areas?

3. What was the ultimate result of 1944's Greater London plan, in the author's opinion?

If you really want to see urban sprawl, take a look at London.

Yes, it's true that Britain has some of the toughest anti-sprawl measures in the world today. But I mean 19th-century London—the miles and miles of brick row houses in Camberwell and Islington. If sprawl is the outward spread of settlement at constantly lower densities without any overall plan, then London in the 19th century sprawled outward at a rate not surpassed since then by any American city.

London's sprawl was attacked just like sprawl today. Although the middle-class families moving into those row houses were thrilled to have homes of their own, members of the artistic and intellectual elite were nearly unanimous in their condemnation. They castigated the row houses as ugly little boxes put up by greedy speculators willing to ruin the beautiful countryside in order to wrest the last penny out of every square inch of land. They were confident that they would become slums within a generation. The Duke of Wellington spoke for many when he denounced the railroads that made these suburban neighborhoods possible as only encouraging "common people to move around needlessly."

Of course, today these neighborhoods are widely considered to be the very essence of central London, the kind of place that the current elite feels must be protected at all cost from the terrible development going on at the new edge of the city. And so it has gone with every major boom period in urban history, from the ancient Romans until today. As each new group has moved up to newer and better housing by moving out from the central city, there has always been another group of individuals ready to denounce the entire process.

Today, the complaints about sprawl are louder than ever, but as in the past, they are built on an extremely shaky foundation of class-based aesthetic assumptions and misinformation. If history is any guide, some modern anti-sprawl prescriptions will prove as ineffective as the Duke of Wellington's. Others will actually backfire.

Most Basic Facts About Sprawl Are Wrong

Even many of the most basic facts usually heard about sprawl are just wrong. Contrary to much accepted wisdom, sprawl in the U.S. is not accelerating. It is declining in the city and suburbs as average lot sizes are becoming smaller, and relatively few really affluent people are moving to the edge. This is especially true of the lowest-density cities of the American South and West. The Los Angeles urbanized area (the U.S. Census Bureau's functional definition of the city, which includes the city center and surrounding suburban areas) has become more than 25% denser over the last 50 years, making it the densest in the country.

This fact, together with the continued decline in densities in all large European urban areas, coupled with a spectacular rise in car ownership and use there, means that U.S. and European urban areas are in many ways converging toward a new 21st-century urban equilibrium. In short, densities will be high enough to provide urban amenities but low enough to allow widespread automobile ownership and use. The same dynamics are at work in the developing world. Although urban densities there are much higher than anything seen in the affluent West, they are plummeting even faster.

A lack of reliable information underlies many of the complaints against sprawl. Take just one example that is considered by many the gravest charge of all: that sprawl fosters increased automobile use; longer commutes; and more congestion, carbon emissions and, ultimately, global warming.

There is no reason to assume that high-density living is necessarily more sustainable or liable to damage the environment than low-density living. If everyone in the affluent West were to spread out in single-family houses across the countryside at historically low densities (and there is plenty of land to do this, even in the densest European counties), it is quite possible, with wind, solar, biomass and geothermal energy, to imagine a world in which most people could simply decouple themselves from the expensive and polluting utilities that were necessary in the old high-density industrial city. Potentially, they could collect all their own energy on-site and achieve carbon neutrality.

Certainly the remedy usually proposed by the anti-sprawl lobby—increasing densities and encouraging public transit—will not solve the global warming problem. Even if all urban dwellers the world over were brought up to "ideal" urban consumption standards—say, that of a Parisian family living in a small apartment and using only public transportation—it would not reduce energy use and greenhouse emissions, since it would require such large increases in energy use by so many families who today are so poor they can't afford the benefits of carbon-based energy.

Unless we deliberately keep most of the world's urban population in poverty, packing more people into existing cities won't solve anything. The solution is finding better sources of energy and more efficient means of doing everything. As we do this, it is quite possible that the most sustainable cities will be the least dense.

Not a Bad Thing in Itself

But let's assume for a moment that I'm entirely wrong and that sprawl is terrible. Could we stop it if we wanted to?

Garden Cities of Tomorrow

Ebenezer Howard, author of the highly influential 1902 text *Garden Cities of To-Morrow*, spent some time in Chicago and witnessed firsthand Riverside, which influenced his theories. Howard's vision of the garden city was also heavily influenced by the dense urban squalor of the time prevalent in cities such as London. As a result, he proposed a decentralised approach that would see the creation of new towns in the countryside. The towns would be self-contained with a mix of land uses, so that people living within the towns had ease of access to employment, services and the countryside. Although Howard's ideas formed the basis of the development of suburbia, in many ways they were radically different from the model of suburbia that would evolve. Unlike conventional suburbia, which was often characterised as being a bed town for large urban centres that was intrinsically reliant on the urban centre for employment, Howard's towns were self-contained, and would minimise the kind of traffic phenomenon—the long commute—that would come to characterize conventional suburbia. In addition, Howard's concept relied on a mix of housing types and lot sizes, that would help allow for a mix of residents.

Matthew Paetz,
"Sustainable Suburbia—Oxymoron or Realistic Goal?,"
November 2010. www.thesustainabilitysociety.org.nz.

The record is not encouraging. The longest-running and best-known experiment was the one undertaken by Britain starting right after World War II. At that time, the British government gave unprecedented powers to planners to remake cities and took the draconian step of nationalizing all development rights to assure that these plans could be implemented.

The famous 1944 Greater London Plan, for example, envisioned a city bounded by a greenbelt. If there happened to be any excess population that couldn't be accommodated within the greenbelt, it was supposed to be accommodated in small, self-contained garden cities beyond the belt.

Did the plan work? In one sense it did: The greenbelt is still there, and some people consider that an aesthetic triumph. But the plan certainly did not stop sprawl. As usual, the planners were not able to predict the future with any accuracy. The population grew, household size declined and affluence rose faster than predicted. Development jumped right over the greenbelt—and not into discreet garden cities, because this policy was soon abandoned.

The ultimate result was that much of southeastern England has been urbanized. Moreover, because of the greenbelt, many car trips are longer than they would have been otherwise, contributing to the worst traffic congestion in Europe.

Finally, since the 1990s, with a new push to try to prevent greenfield development outside the belt, land and house prices have skyrocketed in London, creating an unprecedented crisis in housing affordability there and in virtually every other place that has tried extensive growth management.

Certainly sprawl has created some problems, just as every settlement pattern has. But the reason it has become the middle-class settlement pattern of choice is that it has given them much of the privacy, mobility and choice once enjoyed only by the wealthiest and most powerful.

Sprawl in itself is not a bad thing. What is bad is the concept of "sprawl" itself, which by lumping together all kinds of issues, some real and important and some trivial or irrelevant, has distracted us from many real and pressing urban issues. It also provides the dangerous illusion that there is a silver-bullet solution to many of the discontents created by the fast and chaotic change that has always characterized city life.

> "However costly sprawl has been in the
> past, the stakes are even higher today
> and into the future."

Urban Sprawl Is
Not Beneficial

Pamela Blais

Pamela Blais is a principal and city planner at Metropole Consultants in Toronto, Canada, and author of Perverse Cities: Hidden Subsidies, Wonky Policy, and Urban Sprawl. *In the following viewpoint excerpted from* Perverse Cities, *she argues that urban sprawl—low-density suburban areas—has a long list of costs, including environmental destruction, climate change, declining human health, and depletion of resources. Blais declares that the location of homes is by far the most important factor in reducing energy usage and greenhouse gas emissions—even the efficiency of the greenest home in a car-dependent neighborhood is less than a traditional one in a compact neighborhood. Nonetheless, current planning efforts are not curbing urban sprawl, she contends.*

Pamela Blais, "1: The Price of Sprawl," *Perverse Cities: Hidden Subsidies, Wonky Policy, and Urban Sprawl*, UBC Press, 2010, pp. 1–4. This excerpt is reprinted with permission of the publisher from *Perverse Cities* by Pamela Blais. Copyright © University of British Columbia Press, 2010. All rights reserved by publisher.

As you read, consider the following questions:

1. Why are the stakes of urban sprawl higher now and for the future, as stated by Blais?

2. How does Blais back her claim that household-related transportation creates more greenhouse gases than operating the house itself?

3. How should efforts to address urban sprawl be refocused, in Blais's view?

Sprawl has been lamented for decades. It is usually discussed in terms of its costs, and there is a long list of these: more expensive road, sewer, and water networks; loss of farmland and natural open space; air pollution and related illnesses, such as childhood asthma; excessive commuting and obesity; car accidents; policing; inner-city decline; socioeconomic segregation; isolation of non-drivers; unattractive landscapes; and more. However costly sprawl has been in the past, the stakes are even higher today and into the future. This is because, first, the scale of sprawl itself is increasing; second, the impacts per unit of sprawl are also increasing; and third, the world is changing in a way that makes sprawl issues even more critical now than they have been in the past.

As in other countries, population growth in Canada is increasingly concentrated in cities and, especially, the largest urban regions. Nearly 90 percent of the nation's population growth between 2001 and 2006 occurred in metropolitan areas. Now almost half of Canada's population is concentrated in its six major urban regions. The vast majority of population and employment growth is taking place in outer suburbs, in the form of low-density, single-use suburbs on former farms or natural areas. The amount of land required for each person and job has been increasing. The Canadian urban population grew 45 percent between 1971 and 2001. The amount of urbanized land grew 96 percent during the same period, indicating that we are using more and more land per person.

Levels of car ownership are rising, along with distances driven per car. The number of motor vehicles in Canada has increased from about 11 million in 1975 to almost 19 million in 2004. In the Toronto area alone, it is projected that the number of vehicles will increase by almost 2 million, reaching 5.6 million by 2031. Since 1989 in Canada, urban automobile use has increased by 16 billion passenger-kilometres, reaching 264 billion passenger-kilometres in 2000, while transit travel has remained fairly steady, at 23 billion passenger-kilometres. And, even though fuel efficiency has improved, the move to larger vehicles and SUVs in recent decades, along with increases in truck traffic, has cancelled out these gains in efficiency. Emissions of most pollutants from motorized vehicles have continued to rise.

Twenty-First Century Issues Intimately Related with Sprawl

Moreover, some of the issues that are shaping up to play a major role in the twenty-first century are intimately related to sprawl. Water shortages are one example. Much urban growth is taking place in the very locations with the least water, such as the American Sunbelt, while drought spreads across the agricultural centre of the continent. By disrupting natural hydrological cycles, sprawl contributes to drought. Access to a reliable, affordable water supply will become an ever more critical, city-shaping issue. Food security will be another. Maintaining productive farmland in close proximity to cities is fundamental to providing a secure, local food supply, while averting the substantial greenhouse gas (GHG) emissions associated with long-distance food transport.

Gas prices will continue to rise in the long term as cheaper oil sources become depleted. Rising gas prices intensify the strain on car-dependent neighbourhoods, households, and businesses. Many communities and business districts have been built in such a way that, other than by the automobile, there are very few means of access to and within them. Price peaks in 2008 provided a taste of the potential impact of high gas prices, causing many to rethink their travel, housing, and business location choices. The short-term repercussions of high gas prices were already evident: the decline in the demand for larger vehicles and the closing of the auto plants that produced them. Persistent high prices will see the next phase of altered decision making: people and businesses looking to reduce their need to drive by seeking out urban environments that support walking, cycling, and transit. That is made much more difficult by the kind of urban environment we have built over the last fifty years or so.

Last but not least is the related issue of GHG emissions and global warming. Interestingly, some of the most sprawling nations are those that are either far from meeting their Kyoto [a United Nations protocol aimed at combating global warming] commitments (Canada) or did not sign on to the Kyoto accord to begin with (Australia and the United States). The excessive vehicle travel associated with urban sprawl is a key contributor to GHG emissions. Yet, many government "greening" policies and programs are not addressing the biggest causes of GHG emissions related to cities and urban development. Much of the attention has been focused on programs that aim to reduce consumption within the home—energy-efficient appliances, windows, insulation, furnaces, and so on.

Home Location Far More Important

However, when it comes to reducing energy use and GHG emissions, the location of the home is far more important than are the green features of the house itself. This is because urban location and local context (such as the presence of nearby shops and services, schools and employment opportu-

The Absence of a Sprawl Debate

How might the danger of a single segment of society simply imposing its spatial preferences on others be avoided? First, it is precisely the *absence* of an explicit, values-driven debate about the shape of our built communities that has enabled the dynamics of automobile-oriented sprawl to emerge in metropolitan area after metropolitan area. Without public debate, unexamined assumptions about what constitutes a desirable community hold sway over zoning ordinances, incentive structures, infrastructure provision, and other policy mechanisms that influence the shape of urban development. Such policy measures influence the type of neighborhoods private developers are prone to build, leading developers to continue to build familiar car-centered developments rather than to attempt to offer a broader array of neighborhoods to prospective residents. The all-too-familiar pattern of outward sprawl has lent a spatial monotony to the metropolitan United States that is at odds with the aim of providing a diverse set of spatial environments capable of satisfying a wide variety of individual and community preferences.

Thad Williamson,
Sprawl, Justice, and Citizenship:
The Civic Costs of the American Way of Life,
New York: Oxford University Press, 2010, p. 8.

nities, and the presence of walkable, connected streets) determine how much travel occurs and by what mode. Household-related transportation creates significantly more GHGs than does the running of the home itself. Of the GHGs emitted directly by Canadian households (i.e., in household travel, home heating, lighting, and running appliances), almost two-thirds is related to transportation. Moreover, while the absolute amount of GHG emissions related to running the home has remained relatively constant since 1990, the emissions related to transportation have increased by about 25 percent.

It has also been shown that even the greenest house located in the suburbs, with all the latest energy-saving features *and* an energy-efficient car, consumes more total energy than does a conventional house with a conventional car located in an accessible urban area. This is due to the continued need to drive long distances from the suburban home.

Another study found that simply changing the location of a household from outer suburb to inner area (while holding everything else constant) reduced GHG emissions related to travel by 36 percent. Altering the urban form alone and maintaining a suburban location reduced transportation emissions by 24 percent. But the household located in even the most compact mixed-use suburban neighbourhood still emitted more greenhouse gases than did one in the least compact inner-area neighbourhood. In other words, when it comes to reducing energy use and GHGs, location within the city and local context are critical determinants of GHGs and are substantially more important than are the features of the house. Yet, location and urban form are rarely addressed in GHG reduction strategies, where the focus has been squarely on introducing green features into the house itself.

Planning Not Curbing Urban Sprawl

For all of these reasons, it is increasingly necessary to refocus and redouble efforts to address urban sprawl (by directing growth to central and accessible locations) and to improve the local context of existing and new suburbs. This means retrofitting existing suburbs to diversify the mix of jobs and housing, improving the local accessibility of jobs and services, and increasing transit viability, walking, and cycling. It also means ensuring that newly built suburbs are mixed in terms of housing type and land uses, that they are compact, and that they are designed for modes of travel other than the automobile. Cities are expensive to build but slow and even more expensive to change. In an era of volatile energy costs, climate change, and water shortages, it is critical that new growth take a different tack. Otherwise, we continue to embed severe future problems by building sprawl that will be very difficult and expensive to mitigate.

Unfortunately, to this point, the record on dealing with sprawl is not particularly encouraging. For decades now, planners and others have been trying to put an end to urban sprawl. From the ecosystem planning of the 1970s to sustainable development in the 1980s and, most recently, "smart growth," governments have devoted considerable resources to altering the way in which cities grow. Had these approaches been successful, we ought by now to be living in the kinds of cities described in planning documents—that is, cities that are "healthy," "sustainable," "liveable," "compact," "transit-oriented," "walkable," "mixed use," and "efficient." Clearly, this is not the case.

In other words, planning is not curbing urban sprawl. Urban development continues along the same trajectory as it did before plans for more sustainable and compact development were adopted. Despite the spread of planning across communities, and its increased depth and focus on sustainable urban development patterns, it is not delivering results. Even some of the loudly trumpeted new approaches to city growth, such as new urbanism, have been criticized as merely producing "cuter sprawl."

Periodical and Internet Sources Bibliography

The following articles have been selected to supplement the diverse views presented in this chapter.

Brita Belli	"My Green House Is Bigger than Yours," *E, The Environmental Magazine*, November 1, 2008.
T. Caine	"Sustainability vs. Luxury: Can McMansions Be Green?," *Intercon* (blog), September 21, 2009. http://progressivetimes.wordpress.com.
Wendell Cox	"The Housing Crash and Smart Growth," National Center for Policy Analysis, Policy Report No. 335, June 2011.
Meg Handley	"Are Net-Zero Energy Houses on the Horizon?," *US News & World Report*, August 19, 2011.
Leon Kaye	"New Ideas for Sustainable Architecture in the Americas," *Guardian*, July 5, 2011.
Lake Online	"It's Getting Easier Being Green," September–October 2010. www.thelakeonline.com.
Frank Reale	"Urban Sprawl Is Killing Us, but There's Another Way," *Age*, April 17, 2009.
Sarah Susanka	"From Smaller Houses to Smaller Neighborhoods," *Planning*, October 2010.
Alec Wilkinson	"Let's Get Small," *New Yorker*, July 25, 2011.
Yuka Yoneda	"Inhabit Talks to CodeGreen Solutions' Stephen Rizzo About Greening Existing Buildings," *Inhabitat* (blog), October 26, 2011. http://inhabitat.com.
Fareed Zakaria	"Buildings That Can Breathe," *Newsweek*, August 8, 2008.

OPPOSING
VIEWPOINTS®
SERIES

CHAPTER 3

How Is Eco-Architecture Being Implemented?

Chapter Preface

In recent years, green condominium developments in the United States have attracted attention. The editors of *E, The Environmental Magazine* state, "By their very nature, many condo complexes adhere to some of the most basic tenets of green housing: density, to maximize surrounding open space and minimize buildings' physical and operational footprints; proximity to mass transit, given their typical location in urban areas; and reduced resource use per unit, thanks to shared systems, walls, and common spaces." Additionally, energy-efficient appliances and other sustainable features are built into green condos.

Completed in 2005, Harlem's 1400 on Fifth Avenue is the first condominium in New York City to be green and affordable. "Heralded during construction for its innovative use of filtration and energy conservation features, the building maximizes fresh air, removes allergens, and saves residents at least 37 percent annually in electricity costs," claim Environmental Defense and WE ACT for Environmental Justice in a joint report. The structure itself cuts the filtration of outside air 85 percent more than traditional buildings and filters it twice, and 60 percent of the building is constructed with sustainable or renewable materials. Also, 1400 on Fifth Avenue has a geothermal system that uses water for cooling and heating, eliminating the need for less efficient systems.

But some commentators point out that green condominiums may fall short of sustainability in other areas. Robert Kravitz of Enviro-Solutions, a green cleaning chemicals and tools manufacturer, asserts that many condo managers continue to use bleach, window cleaners, and other products that may compromise the benefits of eco-friendly construction. "A green building must be cleaned and maintained using green cleaning products and systems," argues Kravitz. Referring to a

Harvard University study, Kravitz explains that the ecological and health benefits of sustainable flooring can be lost the first time it is cleaned or maintained with conventional cleaning agents. In the following chapter, the authors present how eco-architecture is practiced by architects, developers, and institutions.

| *"More and more colleges and universities are requiring that all new construction meet LEED standards."*

More College Campuses Are Building Green

Peter W. Bardaglio

In the following viewpoint, Peter W. Bardaglio writes that a growing number of colleges and universities practice green building through Leadership in Energy and Environmental Design (LEED) certification, a ratings system created by the US Green Building Council. From high-performance labs to zero net energy dormitories, he states, educational institutions adopt LEED to conserve resources, help protect the environment, and save money. Research also suggests that green schools experience lower student absenteeism and improved academic performance, he continues. A former university administrator and history professor, Bardaglio is a senior fellow at Second Nature, a nonprofit green organization for colleges and universities, and co-author of Boldly Sustainable: Hope and Opportunity for Higher Education in the Age of Climate Change.

As you read, consider the following questions:

1. As told by Bardaglio, how did the fact that buildings generate nearly 40 percent of all greenhouse gas emissions impact campus construction policies?

2. What are some features of the Smart Home at Duke University, as described by Bardaglio?

3. What are the drawbacks of LEED for colleges and universities, according to Bardaglio?

Even in the midst of the most serious economic downturn since the 1930s, sustainability continues to be a hot topic. New construction is the darling. However, LEED certifications do not come cheap, and retrofitting older buildings is problematic. Is LEED worth it?

Leadership in Energy and Environmental Design (LEED), as certified by the U.S. Green Building Council, has become the coin of the U.S. realm of green buildings. LEED is a rating system with six components: sustainable site development, water savings, energy efficiency, materials and resources selection, indoor environmental quality, [and] innovation [in] design process. In ascending order, the levels of achievement are certified, certified silver, gold, and platinum. It's all in place to encourage building owners to construct, renovate and operate facilities in an environmentally sensitive manner.

In 2005, green building made up roughly two percent of both nonresidential and residential construction in the U.S., with a total value of $10 billion. Today it's grown as high as $49 billion. By 2013, McGraw-Hill Construction estimates it could reach $140 billion. McGraw-Hill's published report concludes, "Green seems to be one area of construction insulated by the downturn."

Green All the Way to the Bottom Line

Why? Several factors are involved, including growing public awareness, aggressive government incentives, and perhaps most important, recognition of the bottom-line advantages afforded by high-performance construction. Going green makes good business sense, especially as energy costs rise. Buildings account for as much as 60 percent of all electricity consumed. On a college campus, buildings are central to a large portion of the operating budget. More and more colleges and universities are requiring that all new construction meet LEED.

Buildings also generate nearly 40 percent of all greenhouse gas emissions. As a result, the American College and University Presidents Climate Commitment encourages signatories, of which there are now 650, to commit to a minimum of LEED silver or its equivalent for new campus construction.

A lesser number of colleges and universities has adopted LEED for existing buildings operations and maintenance (EBO&M), although existing buildings typically represent 95 percent of the building stock on campuses. Upgrading and retrofitting older buildings to improve their energy performance may not have as much curb appeal as a new project, but they offer more opportunity to reduce energy costs and much more potential for lower carbon footprints.

LEED EBO&M is a performance-based system with strong energy and water components that emphasize operational best practices. A pilot program has been launched for institutions that want to implement LEED across the campus rather than on a case-by-case basis. For example, an institutional policy that mandates green cleaning products can establish a LEED points baseline for the entire campus.

Certifiable, Rather than Certified

Administrative fees accompany LEED designation. On new projects some campuses are foregoing LEED certification and are settling for the designation "LEED certifiable," which means that a project meets LEED standards, but does not incur the expense of going through the documentation process.

The possible downside is that the project team may not be as rigorous when it's not subject to third-party verification.

"LEED is any institution's insurance policy that green building standards are being met and verified by a third party," says Brian Malarkey, executive vice president of Kirksey, a Houston-based architectural firm. "Having worked on millions of square feet of LEED projects, I am here to tell you that sometimes the only thing preventing cutting out a particular green feature is the potential loss of LEED certification credits and a resulting rating that's lower than desired."

Malarkey, who heads up Kirksey's eco-services division, also adds, "Bragging about your green buildings without this third-party certification can sound hollow, especially to savvy students, faculty, and researchers."

What Does LEED Certification Cost?

As the talent pool of LEED-aware firms deepens, the extra cost of achieving and documenting LEED has declined significantly. Kirksey estimates that its average LEED premium is only 1.14 percent of the overall construction cost. Even the cost of going platinum has flattened out, provided it is an explicit goal from the outset.

Ithaca College opened a platinum park center in 2008, which incurred a premium cost of less than 5 percent, according to vice president for finance and administration Carl Sgrecci. "Building in these sustainable features may add a few percentage points to the cost today, but we will quickly recoup the investment with a facility that's less costly to operate each year," he says. "And the investment will yield returns for the life of the building."

The business case for green buildings makes so much sense to Sgrecci that he urged the college to also shoot for platinum with its new administrative center. The $25 million, 55,000-

Apply Campus Scale

Due to the multibuilding nature of college campuses, institutions can benefit from approaching green building construction, not from an individual building perspective, but at the campus-scale level. Campuses should identify "base credits" that could apply to all projects thereby facilitating multi-project certification. Integrating LEED [Leadership in Energy and Environmental Design] into the design standards and specifications, for example, would enable every project to achieve associated credits. Keeping documentation on file for every LEED project and sharing information across projects will help to streamline the certification process.

Campus buildings often share common infrastructure, such as utilities management, energy sources, and transportation. Targeting improvements in these areas facilitates campus greening and may contribute to securing credits for the individual buildings seeking LEED certification. Some credits can also be achieved by implementing campus-wide policies and procedures (e.g., such as materials procurement or recycling), which may already be in place as part of a campus-wide greening effort.

When using the LEED framework, it is important to distinguish between credits that will be pursued on a project basis and those that the university should implement campus-wide.

US Green Building Council,
"A. Apply Campus Scale,"
Roadmap to a Green Campus, 2011.

square-foot building, opened in April [2009], and it may make Ithaca College the only campus with two LEED platinum buildings.

Building Usage Makes a Difference

Among academic buildings, the toughest nuts by far to crack are the science labs, very energy intensive because of ventilation and exhaust requirements. In fact, labs consume four to six times more energy than the average office building. Many labs exhaust the entire internal volume of the building more than 10 times per hour.

Classroom and office buildings recirculate air, exhaust a small amount of conditioned air, and operate 50 to 80 fewer hours per week than a lab building. In large research universities, energy use in labs makes up as much as two-thirds of campus electricity consumption.

Nevertheless, a number of high-performance labs have come online in recent years. One such is Weill Hall at Cornell University, which opened in October 2008. The $162 million, 263,000-square-foot life sciences building has a green roof that absorbs rainwater, incorporates natural lighting, and uses 30 percent less energy than comparable buildings. It is one of only six university laboratory buildings to have achieved LEED gold certification.

Green residence halls are cropping up on campus, and they prove very popular with students. The Home Depot Smart Home at Duke University is a 10-person residence hall for green living and learning that achieved LEED platinum certification in June 2008. It was designed by students and advisers, and the 6,000-square-foot building is the first platinum residence hall on any campus. It's also spawned an undergraduate discipline involving more than 100 students.

The Smart Home incorporates a green roof, solar cells, rainwater cisterns, and sophisticated digital electronics. Its fiber-optic network sports the fastest Internet access on the campus, about 40 gigabytes per second. Workshops adjacent to the living areas enable students to experiment with and deploy new technology, while wall panels in every room open easily so that students can add features.

Unity College in Maine has provided its president with a net zero energy house. With solar panels on its roof, the house sits on a concrete pad that retains heat in the winter and helps keep the well-insulated house cool in the warmer months. South-facing windows, all triple-glazed and argon-filled, provide natural light. Low-flow water fixtures, compact fluorescents, and high-efficiency appliances and mechanical systems further minimize the house's carbon footprint.

Unity College president Mitchell Thomashow is an environmental scholar, and his wife Cindy is executive director of the college's Center for Environmental Education. They moved into the new 1,900-square-foot residence in fall 2008. "Unity House is more than just a sustainable solution," blogs Thomashow. "It's a wonderful educational opportunity. We are hoping that the countless visitors to the house will be impressed, inspired, and motivated to live similarly." The architect, Hilary Harris of Bensonwood Homes, worked with a budget of $200 per square foot to demonstrate that a platinum home can be built at an affordable price.

Sick Buildings

Thanks to media coverage we know poorly designed and operated "sick buildings" can cause serious health problems. But the positive impact of green buildings on their occupants is less well known. A growing body of research suggests that the occupants of LEED-certified buildings experience a higher satisfaction level, better health, and improved personal productivity. A 2003 study by the Federal Energy Management Program, for example, found that such buildings resulted in productivity increases of 6 percent to 16 percent.

What about the impact of green buildings on student learning? Few studies have as yet been reported in higher education. K–12 findings suggest substantial positive benefits. Turner Construction released a 2005 survey of 665 school construction executives. Of those involved with green schools, more than 70 percent reported that these new facilities reduced student absenteeism and improved student performance.

Any Drawbacks?

There are drawbacks. A "Campus Application Guide" for LEED colleges and universities does not adequately deal with issues such as transportation, central plants and sites. In addition, as Brian Malarkey is quick to observe, LEED has yet to deal with total life cycle issues, "an important topic considering higher education builds and owns for the long run." The LEED checklist format also imposes limitations. It's easy to "get seduced by 'chasing credits' and lose sight of the larger green goals of a project," notes Malarkey.

Yet there is no question that LEED has transformed the market. And LEED now has a competitor. Green Globes, developed by the Oregon-based Green Building Initiative, positions itself as a more economical alternative to LEED. Like LEED, Green Globes employs a 100-point system, although the applicant can determine that certain points are not relevant to a project. One to four globes are issued, based on the percentage of applicable points achieved.

Green Globes registration and certification fees are significantly less than those for LEED. Total registration and verification cost runs between $5,000 and $7,000 for any project. Green Globes keeps certification costs down by not using a specialized consultant, instead providing a web-based self-assessment tool.

Both LEED and Green Globes grew out of the Building Research Establishment Environmental Assessment Method (BREEAM), launched in the United Kingdom in 1990. BREEAM is the most widely used assessment method outside the U.S. and can be used for a single project or a portfolio of projects both within and across national boundaries.

More flexible than LEED, BREEAM is more adaptable to local circumstances. BREEAM Gulf, for example, places considerable emphasis on water, a critical issue in the Middle East. BREEAM UK focuses more on energy. Desiring to counter the perception that LEED is a one-size-fits-all system, the latest version of LEED, released in April, began to move in a similar direction.

Meanwhile, Rick Fedrizzi, CEO [chief executive officer] and founding chairman of the U.S. Green Building Council, says with no equivocation: "Going backwards after this point in time is simply not an option."

> "The ways education administrators are making their buildings more environmentally friendly are as varied as schools themselves."

More School Campuses Are Building Green

Jonathan Hiskes

In the following viewpoint, Jonathan Hiskes asserts that more primary and secondary schools build green for the ecological, financial, and human benefits. The growing number of sustainable construction and retrofitting projects taking place at schools across the country, he writes, has been a boon to the hard-hit construction industry. Green buildings not only have a solid return on investment for school districts, but also lead students and staff to perform better in these healthier, ecologically friendly campuses and classrooms, Hiskes contends. The author is a correspondent for Sustainable Industries, *a magazine focusing on green businesses, and a former staff writer for the ecological news site* Grist.

As you read, consider the following questions:

1. What do environmentally sound school projects represent to the construction industry, according to the author?

2. What does the Environmental Protection Agency claim about the impact of poor indoor air quality and children?

3. What is Hiskes's opinion about the role of schools and green building?

When students rush into the new Finn Hill Junior High in Kirkland, Wash., on the first day of school this fall [in 2011], they will be greeted by the "Finn Hill Family," a collection of glass figurines designed by a local artist. LEDs inside each sculpture will be wired to controls that measure the electricity, heat and water use of a particular classroom cluster. The more energy and water students conserve, the brighter their figurines will shine.

As they compete to be the best and brightest, the students gain a visual symbol for the energy literacy the school wants to teach. And the Lake Washington School District enlists several hundred allies in managing the energy costs of its 120,000-square-foot building.

This spring, builders are installing a ventilation system that recaptures waste heat as well as tightly sealed walls of insulated panels and a rooftop photovoltaic array. Architects at the Seattle firm Mahlum designed the project to be 65 percent more energy efficient than typical schools in the area, making the case to taxpayers that investments made now will save in operating costs over the building's 40-to 50-year lifetime. "It's a great approach," says Principal Victor Scarpelli, who has become a green-building enthusiast as construction has proceeded. "If we can spend money today and save in the future, we can invest in teachers and resources and give our children the best education possible."

Finn Hill Junior High sits at the vanguard of a green schools building boom driven by federal stimulus spending, local school bonds and education leaders looking to slash energy costs. As the recession-racked construction industry continues to suffer the burst of the housing bubble, green school projects offer a bright spot for builders and designers. Data research company McGraw-Hill Construction estimates that such projects totaled $16 billion last year—up from $9 billion in 2008. That's more than a third of all school construction activity.

"This opportunity is big in California, and it's virtually untapped in the rest of the U.S.," says Bill Kelly, California managing director for SunPower, the Silicon Valley photovoltaic module maker and developer. He estimates that schools in the Golden State alone have the potential to host more than a gigawatt of solar power. "School facilities are some of the biggest public facilities in any state or city."

The ways education administrators are making their buildings more environmentally friendly are as varied as schools themselves. The Mount Diablo Unified School District in the San Francisco Bay Area, for instance, inked a $60 million deal with SunPower to install its high-tech solar panels at 51 schools and facilities this year.

Manassas City Public Schools in Virginia plans to spend $24 million upgrading schools with high-efficiency roofs and heating and cooling systems. The private Epiphany School in Seattle opened last fall with a garden for students to grow food and an off-the-grid ventilation system. When the sun shines, solar-powered rooftop fans suck hot air out of classrooms through a set of chimneys, cooling the building without external power.

For the construction industry, environmentally sound school projects offer rare opportunities during the economic downturn. But planners and builders will have to make the case that their projects serve both students who use them and school district budgets.

Despite the green building boom, education construction fell 36 percent in square footage over the past two years, according to Kim Kennedy, manager of forecasting for McGraw-

Hill Construction. That's less dramatic than the 57 percent drop for commercial and industrial projects in 2009, but it's far from rosy.

Kennedy expects the educational market to decline for at least one more year. "The institutional side is hit with a lag because it's more tied to government expenditures," she says. "We're probably going to see another decline in 2011 for education, whereas the commercial market will already have started to recover in 2011."

While money for green building projects has been flowing, other hurdles will remain beyond this year. Tax bonds approved before the recession fund many current projects, and gaining community approval for future projects will be more difficult during a slow economic recovery. States confronting multibillion-dollar budget deficits will offer limited support. And a key source of capital over the last two years—the American Recovery and Reinvestment Act—has already begun drying up.

Stimulating Retrofits

Two years ago, Judy Marks, director of the non-profit National Clearinghouse for Educational Facilities, took on the task of helping school districts figure out which parts of the stimulus were available for construction and renovation. She says the bulk of funds came through two low-interest lending programs.

In December, Congress extended one of those sources, Qualified School Construction Bonds, in its 11th-hour tax bill. The other main source—Build America Bonds, which provided $179 billion for various public projects—expired at the end of 2010.

Marks has watched stimulus funds make the education market increasingly attractive to builders and designers. "There was no stimulus for hotels or office buildings," she says. "But many school districts made the decision to go forward because of the availability of this money."

With stimulus funds already tapering off, new school construction will depend on the health of the economy. Repair and renovation work, however, should remain steady. Roofs and heating and cooling systems wear out on their own schedules, after all.

And data show retrofits are taking up an increasing share of the schools market: While school construction declined 18 percent in square footage last year, it dropped only eight percent in total spending. Those figures tell McGraw-Hill Construction that more projects are focusing on improving existing schools.

"The renovation market has held up much better than the new construction market," says McGraw-Hill Construction economist Lindsay Hogan.

That's driven in part by incentives for improving the energy performance of schools. For instance, California's Energy Efficiency Financing program makes loans of up to $3 million available for schools to cut their energy footprints.

And the state superintendent, Tom Torlakson, directed $848 million in stimulus tax credits to construction projects that emphasize renewable energy and efficiency. "It makes no sense to teach the next generation of California's students in facilities that are relics of the past, powered by energy sources that are out of touch with our state's renewable future," he said in a statement.

Utilities such as Puget Sound Energy offer grants for schools that make efficiency a priority and commit to ensuring buildings perform as they're designed to do. Finn Hill's district received $60,000 for such work.

The Health Factor

But the push for greener schools is about more than finance. The Environmental Protection Agency finds that children are more affected than adults by poor indoor air quality, and studies have linked mold levels and other airborne aggravators to lower student attendance rates and test scores.

Other researchers discovered that excessively hot or cold rooms harm student performance. Still others concluded that excessive background noise, from such things as noisy radiators, cause measurable distraction. Noise affects teachers too: A fifth of teachers reported missing work because of voice strain, according to a 1998 study by University of Iowa speech researchers.

Four years ago these findings prompted the U.S. Green Building Council [USGBC] to introduce a LEED [Leadership in Energy and Environmental Design] for Schools program that places a greater emphasis on indoor air quality and thermal and acoustical comfort. Last fall, USGBC launched a Center for Green Schools to promote the advantages of green schools—healthier students, savings on energy costs and learning opportunities like the Finn Hill sculptures.

"We want green schools to become the norm, not the exception," says Rachel Gutter, director of the Center for Green Schools.

That means expanding the USGBC's audience of architects and building consultants and reaching janitors, facilities directors, school board members and lawmakers who can improve state standards for school buildings, Gutter says. She's helped create the Center's Green Schools Fellowship program that puts 11 full-time sustainability officers in school districts. They spend three years examining ongoing operations, finding ways to promote carpooling, for example, or comparing sources for paper or cleaning products.

There are more than 130,000 public and private schools in the U.S., Gutter notes, so it's not enough just to build the new buildings better.

Still, new construction offers the greatest potential to showcase what's possible.

At Finn Hill in Kirkland, architect Anjali Grant stood in the school's cavernous future computer lab on a January afternoon and motioned to the metal roof—expensive but long lasting. Soon it will support a 400-kilowatt solar array that the school may expand in the future to make the building a net-zero consumer of electricity.

But Grant considers other features more important, such as a heat pump and a ventilation system that captures and re-uses heat from inside air. Her firm learned on an earlier project—Benjamin Franklin Elementary, also in Kirkland—that venting out warm air can blow the energy savings of an otherwise efficient building.

Here, structural insulated panels and triple-glazed windows seal the warmth inside. They were surprisingly good at keeping out the winter chill, even with temporary plywood doors.

The five classroom pods stretch out in southern-oriented rows to catch the most of the area's limited sunlight. In the muddy courtyards outside each pod, landscapers will build rain gardens—shallow depressions of native plants—that will attract birds and wildlife, reduce rain runoff and give teachers an outdoor laboratory.

Polished cement floors (with carpet in some places) will avoid the need for waxing and materials that emit fumes. A red light/green light system in classrooms will tell teachers when the central heat is off and windows may be opened (green) and when to keep them shut (red).

Grant acknowledged that not all school districts can afford features like solar arrays and the long-lasting metal roof, but she says the most important green features carry no extra cost.

"It doesn't cost extra to design for daylight," she says, standing at a long bank of southern windows. "It doesn't cost extra to use non-toxic materials."

And the elements that do cost more pay for themselves over time. A 2006 study by Greg Kats of Capital-E, a national green building firm, found that a two percent increase in initial costs—about $3 per square foot—paid back $10 per square foot in energy and water savings over a building's life span.

Location Matters

But that's all about the interior workings of a school. Advocates of smart growth and walkable neighborhoods argue that the most important issues for sustainable schools are location and how they connect to the surrounding community.

School sites that are woven into compact urban neighborhoods can encourage students to walk—which gives them exercise along with all the environmental advantages of driving less.

Architects and builders typically have less say in a school's location, since districts already have sites in mind. "There's only so much we can do for a suburban neighborhood like this," Grant says of the Finn Hill site. "That's a function of local zoning."

Designers can still make improvements. Grant's plan adds sidewalks to the site and lets pedestrians reach the main entrance without crossing parking lots—something not all school designs have accomplished in the past. The plan also preserves walk-through routes that let neighbors reach the adjacent Finn Hill Park. Safety remains a major priority for school administrators, but school sites shouldn't be fortresses that seal themselves off from their surrounding communities, Grant says.

In fact, it's difficult to imagine communities becoming carbon free without the leadership of schools. Every day one-fifth of Americans go to a school to study or work, giving enormous influence to those institutions and the people who build their facilities. More importantly, many of those students are eager to learn about the world around them—both how it is and how it could be.

The Center for Green Schools sensed this opportunity and began offering curriculum guides and classroom project ideas for teachers. The Finn Hill Family environmental sculpture is unusual, but other schools are adding touch-screen monitors that let students learn about the electricity and water coursing through their buildings.

The Alliance to Save Energy, an efficiency advocacy group born out of the 1970s oil embargoes, launched its own Green Schools Program that trains students to measure their school's energy footprint with light meters and infrared temperature guns and lets them work with teachers to make improvements.

"It's a lot easier to make a difference working with children," program manager Megan Campion says. "I think most 12-year-olds are sort of environmentalists."

| "Hospitals are going green not only to protect the environment but also the health of their patients and staff."

Hospitals Go Green

Karen Sandrick

Karen Sandrick is a writer based in Chicago, Illinois. In the following viewpoint, she maintains that hospitals are adopting green building practices for their environmental benefits and the well-being of patients and staff. Sandrick claims that hospital administrators use Leadership in Energy and Environmental Design (LEED), a voluntary rating system, to ensure building projects are constructed with sustainability. Harkening back to their sunny, naturally ventilated predecessors built a century ago, LEED-certified hospitals combine such designs with energy-conserving technologies, recycled and nontoxic materials, and building features that reduce pollution, she says. The positive impacts on patient health and staff productivity, Sandrick insists, are measurable.

As you read, consider the following questions:

1. How does the energy consumption of hospitals compare to that of commercial buildings, as stated in the viewpoint?

Karen Sandrick, "Hospitals Go Green," *Trustee*, May 2009. Reprinted by permission from *Trustee*, May 2009. Copyright © 2009 by Health Forum, Inc.

2. What evidence does Sandrick provide to back her claim that sunlight improves patient health?

3. How did the construction of Dell Children's Medical Center reuse and recycle waste, as described by Sandrick?

When Children's Hospital of Austin, Texas, first began planning to build an environmentally sustainable replacement facility six years ago [in 2003], the board of trustees felt it was in the best position to explore some key strategic issues. So the hospital wouldn't sink big dollars into capital improvements that might not serve the community into the future, board members concentrated on:

- *How healthy it would be to occupy the building over the long term.* Because of the desire to make use of durable materials, the number and amount of toxins traditionally used in hospital construction have been considerable. "But people have to work in the hospital 24/7, so how do we make sure their health is not compromised because builders don't automatically put in nontoxic types of materials?" says Donna Carter, who chaired the board committee that oversaw the design and construction of the new hospital.

- *How a new building project would meet the needs of the local environment.* "We are a community that takes energy conservation and sustainability issues seriously. These concepts are written into the community's goals and objectives toward long-term development. It was the board's role to reflect those community objectives at a focused and strategic level for the hospital," Carter says.

- *How a sustainable hospital would foster the mission of the organization and still keep costs in line.* Children's Hospital is part of the Seton family of faith-based health care facilities whose stewardship responsibilities involve not only financial but environmental health. "We, as board members, can outline how conservation and sustainability meet our hospital mission," Carter says. "We can look at the bottom line and operating costs and make sure everyone understands that sustainability isn't just about the first dollar cost of equipment or materials or even energy operating costs. It has a much broader definition. We, as members of the board, can ask about the advantages of having more control over our energy source and how we consume water."

The replacement facility, which was named Dell Children's Medical Center of Central Texas, opened its doors in 2007, and will most likely become the first children's health care building project to achieve the platinum designation from the Leadership in Energy and Environmental Design (LEED) program of the U.S. Green Building Council.

LEED is a voluntary rating system that ranks building projects and gives award certifications in four levels: certified, silver, gold and platinum. LEED projects must meet green building criteria in five areas: sustainability of the building site; efficiency of water usage; management of energy and atmosphere; choice of building materials; and quality of the indoor environment. Oregon Health & Science University medical center was the first hospital to receive platinum certification in 2007. LEED platinum is the most stringent certification level; building projects must meet at least 52 out of a total 69 points.

Hospital trustees were critical for keeping the focus of the new building on sustainability, says Carter. "Senior management is charged with making sure a building project gets done, that all the programming aspects are met and that it is on time and on budget. The hospital executives are the direct line of communication with the architects and construction managers as a project goes forward. If they are taking on the strategic questions as well, they are not going to get their basic work done," she says.

"It's not that senior management wasn't involved in strategic decisions. But our oversight committee allowed for a point and counterpoint discussion that did not affect the progress of the project. It allowed us to help create a pleasant and uplifting space that goes a long way toward getting a better outcome for everyone, and bottom line, we are after better outcomes," Carter says.

The Growing Sustainability Movement

Ironically, hospitals built more than 100 years ago were more in tune with their environment than many of their modern counterparts. Hospitals that once relied on fresh air and water for healing have, over the decades, morphed into high rises with mechanical air-conditioning and closed-in, dimly-lit spaces. When Bellevue hospital in New York City was first built, it epitomized hospital design principles at the time, which emphasized natural light, natural ventilation and access to fresh water. After many years of expansion, the hospital now occupies 60,000 square feet of floor space on an acre and a half of land and less than 10 percent of it has windows, according to Robin Guenther, who spoke at the Health, Environment, and Economics Workshop sponsored by Green Healthcare Institutions in 2007. Guenther is with Perkins + Will, an architecture firm with offices worldwide.

Hospitals consume large amounts of resources to artificially heat up, cool down and keep the lights burning and use far more environmental resources than other commercial buildings. A majority of health care facilities eat up nearly twice the annual energy total of an average commercial building, says Joe Kuspan, director of design for the Karlsberger architecture firm, Columbus, Ohio, and lead architect on the Dell Children's Hospital project. Hospitals account for roughly

4 percent of the footprint of all commercial buildings in the United States, but they use 8 percent of the energy, he says. Hospitals are resource-intensive buildings because of medical necessity. "You completely knock out someone's immune system to treat them for cancer. You really have to take some strong steps to keep them alive that aren't necessarily energy friendly," Kuspan says.

Unlike office buildings, for example, hospitals cannot save on energy use by recirculating air or drastically reducing lighting, heating and cooling at night. Nor can they take advantage of energy-saving, raised-floor mechanical systems that keep mechanically ventilated air from stratifying in open office environments. "The last thing you want to do is blow air up off the floor into someone's open wound," says Kuspan.

Nevertheless, many new hospitals are adopting energy-efficient principles. Northwestern University's $509 million Prentice Women's Hospital in Chicago, which opened in the fall of 2007, has a 9,500-square-foot green roof and a low-emissivity glass curtain wall system that lets in ample amounts of daylight and controls the amount of energy consumed. And Patrick H. Dollard Health Center, a facility that cares for neurologically and developmentally impaired individuals in Harris, N.Y., incorporated ground source heat pumps. This reduced its energy consumption by 48 percent, according to the U.S. Green Building Council.

Hospitals also are removing pollutants from their interiors and their grounds. Over the last five years, Kaiser Permanente, Oakland, Calif., stopped purchasing and disposing of 40 tons of hazardous materials annually. And Dollard Health Center eliminated polyvinyl chloride finishes and plumbing supplies.

Botsford Hospital in Farmington, Mich., which is scheduled to open in 2009, is green in construction as well as in operation. The hospital's construction firm, Madison, Wis.-based Marshall Erdman & Associates, is recycling drywall construction waste into fertilizer. Drywall accounts for more than

25 percent of the waste from major construction projects that routinely is carted away to landfills, where its principal ingredient, gypsum, releases sulfur and calcium as it decays. Design elements that captured a LEED silver certification will allow Botsford Hospital to use 30 percent less water and 17.5 percent less energy.

An 80-bed, $221 million replacement hospital for two hospitals in the Mountain States Health Alliance, Johnson City, Tenn., is being designed around energy efficiency, conservation and environmental responsibility. The building will lie naturally within the existing terrain and capture sunlight, which ties in not only with energy efficiency, but also with a patient-centered care environment of peace, comfort and support, says CEO Dennis Vonderfecht. Even the parking lot and roof will have green spaces with grass and trees that will remove pollutants, such as asphalt and oil, from rainwater. In turn, the rainwater from the roof will be channeled into falling cascades that run over natural rock along the sides of the building, adds Vonderfecht.

Hospitals are going green not only to protect the environment but also the health of their patients and staff. Increasing numbers of studies show the health benefits of high levels of natural sunlight. In one study, published in *Psychosomatic Medicine* in 2005, patients whose rooms were located on the sunny side of the hospital were perceived to be less stressed and needed 22 percent fewer analgesics while recuperating from elective neck or lower spine surgery than those located on the other side of the hospital.

Green buildings foster health by opting for less toxic materials in adhesives and sealants, carpets, composite woods and paints and by controlling indoor chemicals and pollutants at their source. Green buildings also allow more daylight and greater control of light levels and glare, and they regularly monitor the release of carbon dioxide in the operation of heating and air-conditioning systems. By giving occupants more control over ventilation, temperature and lighting, employee productivity increases anywhere from 0.5 percent to 34 percent in green buildings, reported Gregory Kats in a 2003 report from Capital-E, a Washington, D.C.-based consultant firm that specializes in the clean energy industry.

The cost of building an environmentally sustainable building is higher than it is for a standard structure. The cost premium is about 2 percent greater, averaging between $3 and $5 a square foot. However, the savings in energy, emissions, water use, operations and maintenance, plus the gains in productivity and health, have a net return of $50 to $65 a square foot, Kats concluded.

Green buildings commonly consume 30 percent less energy by decreasing their use of electricity, particularly during high-energy demand periods, and generating their own power on-site, according to Kats. Additionally, hospitals cited for environmental excellence by Hospitals for a Healthy Environment in 2007, which is now a part of Practice Greenhealth, reported significant savings from recycling alone. The University of Michigan hospitals and health centers, Ann Arbor, saved $236,000 in 2006 by recycling 1,350 kilograms of elasticized arm or leg compression sleeves. Dartmouth-Hitchcock Medical Center, Lebanon, N.H., saves approximately $48,000 per year by recycling xylene and alcohol.

Dell Children's Medical Center

The $200 million Dell Children's Medical Center of Central Texas is far more spacious than its predecessor, Children's Hospital of Austin. It has a total of 475,000 square feet, three times more than the facility it replaced, as well as 32 emergency department bays, 10 clinical imaging suites, six operating rooms, 14 recovery rooms, and additional services such as conference and education centers, a rehabilitation gym, a theater, and a play area for patients' siblings.

The Economic Argument for Creating Sustainable Facilities

There appears to be little doubt that there will be an increase in the initial capital cost of a project when developing it as a sustainable model. However, these additional costs can be offset over the life of the facility. Achieving a sustainable design can typically add 6–12% to overall capital costs, depending on the size of the facility, how realistic the initial budget is, client expectations, site constraints, the commitment and inventiveness of the team engaged in the process, and the ability of the procurement route to support a whole-life cost approach. What is clear from the modelling that we have carried out is that, by adopting a holistic approach to the design and evaluation process, solutions become mutually supportive across a number of aspects of sustainability. The whole then becomes greater than the sum of the parts in terms of the savings generated over time, as well as the less easily identifiable clinical, carbon, staff and societal benefits.

Rosemary Glanville and Phil Nedin,
"Chapter 12: Sustainable Design for Health,"
Investing in Hospitals of the Future, Copenhagen, Denmark:
World Health Organization, 2009, p. 244.

The hospital makes ample use of natural sunlight, and it mirrors the local ecology. It has a hub-and-spoke design that channels natural light throughout the facility and seven interior courtyards that mimic the ecosystems in the hospital's surrounding area. Interior paints and adhesives were used that have no or only small amounts of volatile organic compounds, such as linoleum secured with green-labeled adhesives and carpeting and backing made of recycled materials.

During construction, work crews were careful to reuse or recycle waste. Contractors recycled 70 percent of project waste, including 35,000 tons of asphalt that was removed from the building site, pulverized and used as a base for parking areas. Contractors also decreased the use of cement, which releases elevated levels of carbon dioxide.

In cooperation with Austin Energy, Dell Children's Medical Center operates an energy cogeneration plant to conserve energy use. The cogeneration plant, which supplies energy directly to the hospital, is 2.5 times more efficient and, more important from a health care standpoint, provides clean power, Kuspan says.

"The IT department has already taken note of the fact that their equipment is not breaking down. There are no power spikes, which shorten the life of high-technology equipment. When you think of a hospital, which has $2 million MRIs [Magnetic Resonance Imaging] and other incredibly sensitive equipment, you want to have reliable power," Kuspan explains.

The cogeneration plant also saves on energy costs. The plant cost $18 million to build, but it saves the hospital $6 million by redirecting natural gas that otherwise would be sent up the smokestack to make steam to power the hospital as well as other buildings on campus, including a Ronald McDonald House, medical office buildings and a pediatric research facility, Kuspan says.

Building according to LEED principles did add to the cost of construction, but it wasn't as expensive as CEO Robert Bonar originally thought. The hospital will recoup its investment in green building strategies in about five years, largely because of savings on energy usage. For hospitals that may be contemplating green building but fear the extra costs, Bonar advises caution and careful analysis.

"There's nothing at all wrong with being concerned about the cost. In fact, a healthy skepticism is good. But I would tell people to at least take a look at it in more detail because they may be able to make up that extra cost in four or five years and then some."

A green building project also may resonate with the local community. The original goal for Dell Children's Medical Center's fund-raising campaign for capital construction was $50 million. Once the project went green, the campaign raised an additional $36 million. "It became an interesting interaction with the business community in Austin, who thought by and large, it was a great idea," Bonar says. "When I showed them charts and graphs that we could recoup our investment in five years, they became even more interested. So the project helped our philanthropy as well."

By maintaining the link between the project and the community, the board of Dell Children's Medical Center showed how a health care facility fits within the larger health care universe. "One of the biggest issues was how to construct a building so patient flow would facilitate and maintain continuity of care," says Bonar.

As an example, a common problem in pediatrics is the kind of life children return to once they are discharged from the hospital. "How can we run these kids through our system so there is a checkpoint before they leave?" Bonar asks. "How can we be sure that, even though we've given them a prescription and a two-day supply of drugs, that they will actually get the medication they need so they don't come back through the emergency room and are readmitted?"

On the surface that issue would seem to have little to do with a building project. But, Bonar says, it influences the design of the portals of entry and exit within the hospital as well as the community at large. Out of discussions with board members rose the Children's Optimal Health initiative, which includes hospital and other health care providers, schools, police and social service agencies in a collaborative effort to improve the health status of area children.

The Children's Health Express, a van that has been converted for use as mobile exam rooms, is now on the road four days a week to provide checkups, immunizations and follow-up care.

"It's funny how things began as a sort of germ and flourished in the discussions of our board building oversight committee," says Bonar. "This was started by trustees asking questions and advancing ideas and propositions for the building of the children's hospital."

It rose from the trustees' stewardship. "And that doesn't just mean stewardship of the organization's financial status," says Bonar. "It also means stewardship of things that are usable and exhaustible and part of that is the environment and the health of the children who live in it."

| "Greenwashing is at the forefront of the new risks that must be faced and incorporated into risk management plans by participants at every level of the construction industry."

False Claims of Green Building Practices Create Confusion

Jay B. Freedman

Jay B. Freedman warns in the following viewpoint that building practices and products may be greenwashed, wherein sustainability claims are intentionally or unintentionally exaggerated or false. Forms of greenwashing, he states, include undisclosed trade-offs that are not environmentally friendly; vague or unsupported claims of natural or organic components; and contractors and designers relying only on advertisements or marketing materials when choosing green products. In addition to favorable press surrounding green building, financial incentives increase the potential for greenwashing, Freedman claims. The author is a partner at Newmeyer & Dillion, a business and real estate law firm in California.

Jay B. Freedman, "Coming Clean: Green Building Brings Risk of Greenwashing," *FMI Quarterly*, vol. 3, 2008, pp. 7–10. Reproduced by permission.

As you read, consider the following questions:

1. What are consumers' attitudes toward green advertising, in the author's view?

2. What real-world example of an undisclosed trade-off does Freedman retell?

3. In what ways are green projects rewarded that can encourage greenwashing, as stated by Freedman?

Like it or not, contractors and those involved in construction across the country must acknowledge the trend toward building green. Celebrities advocate it. Government agencies encourage or mandate it. The media publicizes it. Contractors must anticipate and manage the new risks associated with the design and construction practice. Greenwashing is at the forefront of the new risks that must be faced and incorporated into risk management plans by participants at every level of the construction industry.

Greenwashing is not a new phenomenon. While it may now include a few new tricks, the practice is at least 40 years old and began when corporations tried to improve their public images after the start of the modern environmental movement. For instance, in 1969 public utilities spent more than $300 million on advertising, more than eight times what they spent on the antipollution research they were touting in their ads. Whether the utilities were trying to mislead the public is uncertain, but it is certain that they were trying to create a green image.

Leading Factors

Though the times have changed, the need for good public relations and marketing remains. Given the media buzz and government mandates concerning green building, contractors, designers and others involved in the construction process have a strong interest in putting an environmentally friendly face on their services, products and experiences. Even a cursory review of *Engineering News-Record* and other industry trade publications will find many ads for green products, from concrete countertops to low-VOC [volatile organic compounds] sealants to tankless water heaters.

Unfortunately, the green claims may be mistakes, exaggerations or outright lies. To further compound the risk, consumers are generally skeptical towards green advertising, distrusting the corporations behind the ads. A recent survey of 6,000 consumers found that more than 20% of those surveyed said they never believe claims made in green advertisements, according to a story about the perils of greenwashing aired on NBC's *Today* show. Two-thirds of the survey's respondents said they only believe the claims sometimes. With an already litigious society, allegations of greenwashing may become a litigation lightning rod. Coincidently, jury research indicates that two-thirds of jurors agree that it is appropriate to award damages against corporate defendants even though the corporation is not at fault.

How It Occurs

Intentional or accidental, greenwashing encompasses a wide variety of conduct and arises for a variety of reasons. At its heart, however, greenwashing involves some form of flawed communication, ranging from actual advertising materials to statements contained in building permit applications. The most subtle forms of greenwashing involve so-called hidden trade-offs such as advertising a product as being energy efficient without disclosing that it contains environmentally unfriendly materials. Another example is advertising the use of recycled materials during construction without disclosing that the materials are trucked in across four other states. In both instances, the advertised green feature is offset or negated by an undisclosed environmentally unfriendly practice.

Of course, the advertiser may not be aware of the undisclosed trade-off. The hypothetical contractor that contracts to buy recycled materials may not know the source of the materials. In one real-world example, an owner seeking LEED [Leadership in Energy and Environmental Design] certification sought credits based on the use of regional materials. The owner contracted with a supplier to provide the materials, but did not inform the supplier of the reasons underlying the materials choice. The supplier then substituted another regional material that was first sent out-of-state for processing. In both the hypothetical and real-world examples, the greenwashing could have been avoided if all parties understood the green building purposes.

Similarly, greenwashing can result from ignorance or misunderstanding. Building "green" can mean different things to different people. Some people assume that a green building is energy-efficient, while others believe that it will provide a healthier indoor environment, while still others focus on site selection. To many in the building industry, green means sustainable, which is yet another term subject to multiple meanings. The lack of a generally accepted definition creates a landscape that can foster unintentional greenwashing.

Greenwashing can also be more overt, even intentionally false. It can involve unsupported claims, such as representations of "organic" components without providing any way to check the certification. Some manufacturers certify themselves rather than employ third parties. Greenwashing can involve vague claims, such as advertising that a product is 100% natural, even though natural products can still be hazardous. In fact, these kinds of claims have drawn the attention of the Federal Trade Commission [FTC]. The FTC is currently reviewing its restrictions on environmental marketing claims in response to allegations of false advertising, and new guidelines are expected by the end of 2008. [Proposed revisions issued October 2010 are still under review as of March 2012.]

"The Art of Greenwashing," illustration by Tom Fishburne, Tom.Fishburne.com, 2007. Copyright © 2007 by Tom Fishburne. Reproduced by permission.

In Construction

The most problematic instances of greenwashing may occur in the construction since in this context, it relates to false or misleading claims about the green benefits of component parts. Contractors and designers need to research the alleged benefits and track record of green products prior to using them. They need to read beyond the marketing materials to really understand a product before touting its green benefits. Builders, contractors and design professionals will likely not be able to rely on product advertisements to successfully defend themselves from greenwashing allegations. To the contrary, it is likely that those involved in green building will be held to a higher standard of care.

For example, green contractors have received complaints about acoustics in buildings that use natural ventilation instead of HVAC [heating, ventilation, and air-conditioning] systems. It seems people are used to hearing the familiar buzz of the mechanical ventilation. The market responded with sound-masking systems (i.e., white-noise machines). One such system was advertised as being "green" because it allegedly conserved energy, improved light quality, improved thermal comfort and increased thermal efficiency and controllability. However, all of these claims are subject to allegations of green-washing.

The sound-masking system itself does not conserve energy; it is installed to create background noise when the building's HVAC system is not working. The energy savings are created by the reduced use of the HVAC system. The sound-masking system does not improve light quality. It may be installed in buildings that employ daylighting in connection with natural ventilation, with the natural light improving the light quality. Similarly, thermal comfort, thermal efficiency and thermal controllability are improved by the green aspects of the HVAC system, not the sound-masking system. Nonetheless, the marketing materials promote the sound-masking system as a green product.

In another real-world example, a law firm recognized for its environmental lobbying hired a design team for the firm's new office. The law firm wanted to use the highest green standards, and the design team made several product recommendations based on the team's review of marketing materials. The local press investigated the design and discovered that the proposed systems and products were not as green as claimed. The firm was then accused of greenwashing.

Financial Incentives

In addition to positive press, market conditions have created financial incentives for building green. As the financial incentives increase, so do the incentives to greenwash at all stages of the construction process. Many local agencies have enacted green building programs that reward green projects. Contractors can receive expedited permits, shortened plan review or reduced permit fees if they build green projects. As a result, they may be inclined to exaggerate the green aspects of their project. At the same time, green projects may be subject to heightened scrutiny because of the financial incentives involved. At least for the next few years, all parties should expect to face additional questions. Contractors should properly document all aspects of their green projects so they can provide the requested answers. If a contract requires low-VOC paint, the contractor, designer and subcontractor should all be able to prove that low-VOC paint was, in fact, used. If a project promises to reduce water usage by 35%, the parties will need not only to document the reduction going forward but also should consider demonstrating that the technology involved has an established track record.

Greenwashing is currently a buzzword in a skeptical society. Those in the construction industry should expect that promises of greener projects and products will be closely evaluated by the buying public and that allegations of greenwashing will be publicized. However, attention to detail, proper communication and adequate research, combined with awareness of the more subtle aspects of greenwashing, can reduce or eliminate much of the risk.

"For the most part, green building standards are all about helping you become a little less bad."

Current Green Building Certification Is Not Enough

Jason F. McLennan, as told to Jonathan Hiskes

In the following viewpoint, Jason F. McLennan discusses with Jonathan Hiskes his view that current green building standards fall short of achieving sustainability for future generations. In place of Leadership in Energy and Environmental Design (LEED), the widely used voluntary rating system, McLennan advocates much stricter standards for new construction, including that structures produce all their own energy, use on-site water, avoid listed toxic materials, build on previously developed land, and account for beauty in design. McLennan is chief executive officer of the Cascadia region Green Building Council and author of The Philosophy of Sustainable Design. *Hiskes is a correspondent for* Sustainable Industries, *a magazine focusing on green businesses, and a former staff writer for the ecological news site Grist.*

Jonathan Hiskes, "The Case for Super-Ambitious Living Buildings. A Talk with Jason McLennan," Grist.org, September 30, 2010. Copyright © 2010 Grist Magazine, Inc. All rights reserved. Reproduced by permission.

As you read, consider the following questions:

1. How does McLennan respond to the concern that energy should be a top priority in green building?

2. What is McLennan's view of toxics and the current industrial system?

3. In McLennan's opinion, what does the 1970s reveal about beauty as a factor in innovative design and technology?

Four years ago [in 2006], Seattle architect Jason [F.] McLennan introduced the Living Building Challenge, posing the question, "What if every single act of design and construction made the world a better place?" McLennan proposed a building standard that calls for new structures to produce all of their own energy and use only water that falls on-site. Builders must use sustainably sourced materials and avoid a "red list" of toxic materials including asbestos, mercury, and PVC [polyvinyl chloride]. They must build on previously developed sites and meet measurements of livability, social equity, and beauty.

The Living Building Challenge's seven performance standards—which McLennan calls "petals," evoking the elegance and efficiency of a flower—are far more demanding than even the highest level of LEED [Leadership in Energy and Environmental Design], the most widespread green building certification. McLennan knows that the vast majority of developers will go about their business as usual. Yet 70-some projects are striving to rise to the Living Buildings standard, including the 11-story Oregon Sustainability Center in Portland and the Bullitt Foundation building in Seattle (none has been completed and certified thus far). I chatted recently with McLennan, CEO of the Cascadia region Green Building Council, about the green building movement he's working to build.

A New, More Stringent Standard

Jonathan Hiskes: There were already green building standards, most notably LEED, when you launched the Living Building Challenge in 2006. What was the need for a new, much more stringent standard?

Jason McLennan: There was—and continues to be—no standard that helps people understand where we ultimately need to head.

For the most part, green building standards are all about helping you become a little less bad. Given what we know about environmental issues around the globe, we need to move much quicker.

We did this as a way of changing the nature of this discussion, to motivate the leading thinkers to push further faster. It's a certification program, but it's also a philosophy, and a market-changing tool, and an advocacy tool. It was the classic reason you put something on the market: because there is nothing quite like it out there.

If climate change is our most pressing ecological threat, one could argue that energy should trump just about every other consideration for buildings. But it's just one of the seven performance areas or "petals," in your standard.

Yeah, but we require net zero energy for all buildings, which is not a small thing to achieve.

We agree that climate change is our paramount, signal issue. But that doesn't mean that other issues are not important, or that they may prove to be less important in the long run. History is filled with examples of things we thought were the top priority turning out not to be the top. In fact, what the environmental movement should teach us above all else is that the moment we take a singular view and try to solve a problem in isolation, that's the moment we cause problems for ourselves in other areas.

No New Sites

One complaint about LEED is that it doesn't give enough priority to where a structure is actually sited—walkable, compact areas versus car-dependent places. How did you approach your location requirement?

We don't allow new sites. You have to build on previously developed places—either brownfields or grayfields. We're basically saying if it wasn't developed by 2007, then it's off-limits. So all farmland stays farmland, all forest land stays forest land, etc. There are always exceptions in life, so there are exceptions in this system, but for 99 percent of projects this holds true. Our cities are filled with underdeveloped sites and poorly developed buildings. It's time for them to be properly developed. We have enough land—we don't need to expand anymore.

We also have another big imperative for car-free living. It's not saying you can't have a car, but that every decision on a development has to move us toward the ability to have a car-free society. So the project cannot lower the density of a site. If you tear down a ten-story building, you can't replace it with a two-story building.

Does that make for a very urban, centralized focus?

There's a big, important place in our society for towns and villages. It's not just supercities. That's important when you start thinking about food. But we do need to stop building on farmland and the few wild places that remain.

The third area I wanted to talk about is toxics. There's a tendency to see the climate threat as distinct from environmental health issues, but it sounds like you want to approach them all together.

We have to tackle it all together. The point of our whole movement is to create abundance of life, and a healthy ecosystem for all future generations. We have a current industrial system where nobody knows what's in our materials, and there's no plan for where they go with those chemicals when their life span is over. That's a pretty bad system. So as long as we need to eat and breathe, toxics should be an important thing to watch for. And our list is not long enough, in any sense.

It's also strategic: We're trying to pick on a certain group of chemicals that don't have to be in our building materials and are particularly nasty. Over time, we'll add to our list. I hope these things are all banned just like we've banned certain things like asbestos and lead. But we haven't even really abandoned asbestos and lead, we've just abandoned some applications.

Beauty as Part of the Framework

You've also got an imperative for beauty—how does that work?

We are trying to make sure that people want Living Buildings, that they want solar buildings, and they want to build energy efficiency. For that to happen they have to be attracted to the solutions. The best technology in the world is useless if it's not implemented. So people have to be demanding this stuff.

We can look at setbacks from the 1970s on really innovative technologies and designs that were just really bad to look at, and uncomfortable to be in. Designers didn't always understand that people need to be comfortable while they're doing the right thing, and they need to like it. It set the movement back as it turned a lot of people off. So we include "good design" and beauty as part of a holistic framework. Sometimes the most important things are things that are not easily measured.

So who decides if a building makes the cut for beauty?

We're not actually judging beauty. We're bringing up beauty as a topic that is important. So the architect and owner have to write essays that describe why this building is beautiful, what was done to create a wonderful place. Then the occupants of the building also have to weigh in. It changes the nature of the discussion. We're saying these issues matter, and even if we don't know how to measure them.

So who takes on this challenge? How many current projects are under way?

A surprisingly large number of people. The number is in the 70s, with some attrition and some new projects coming up. There are a lot of projects that don't register because they want to see how far they can get before they register. Or they don't register in case they fail, they don't want it to be known. So the real number is considerably higher than 70.

It tends to be people who get the problem and the challenge that we're in, and they want to be a part of a solution. We certainly get those who see this as a big marketing opportunity. There are already so many LEED buildings, so how do you distinguish yourself by going further? I mean, Americans love a healthy competition. There are a lot of people who read about it and say, "Yeah, this is how we should be doing building. And if we don't achieve it all, at least we tried."

Periodical and Internet Sources Bibliography

The following articles have been selected to supplement the diverse views presented in this chapter.

Carol Ann Campbell   "Even Hospitals Are Going Green," NJ.com, February 23, 2009. www.nj.com.

Wendy Koch   "Eco-Friendly Schools Offer Students Fresh Lessons," *USA Today*, October 20, 2008.

Robert Kravitz   "The Greenwashed Green Condo," *CondoBusiness*, April 2009.

Christine MacDonald   "Green or Greenwashed?," *E, The Environmental Magazine*, March 7, 2011.

Martin C. Pedersen   "Inside the Green Toolbox," *Metropolis*, October 2009.

Tristan Roberts   "The Nine Types of Greenwashing," Building Green.com, June 23, 2011. www.buildinggreen.com.

Shari Shapiro   "Greenbashing—Greenwashing's More Evil Twin," GreenBiz.com, August 5, 2009. www.greenbiz.com.

Sierra   "America's Coolest Schools," September/October 2011.

Josh Stephens   "Starchitecture and Sustainability: Hope, Creativity, and Futility Collide in Contemporary Architecture," Planetizen, November 1, 2009. www.planetizen.com.

Esther Walker   "Too Cool for School: Britain's Most Eco-Friendly Building," *Independent*, April 10, 2008.

CHAPTER 4

How Can Eco-Architecture Be Encouraged in the Future?

Chapter Preface

Established in 1990 by the Building Research Establishment (BRE), BRE Environmental Assessment Method (BREEAM) is the voluntary rating system for green buildings in the United Kingdom, comparable to the Leadership in Energy and Environmental Design (LEED) in the United States. "The measures used represent a broad range of categories and criteria from energy to ecology," states BRE. "They include aspects related to energy and water use, the internal environment (health and well-being), pollution, transport, materials, waste, ecology, and management processes." More than 110,000 buildings are BREEAM certified and about 500,000 more are registered.

The following are the four areas of evaluation in the rating system: BREEAM rating benchmarks, BREEAM environmental weightings, minimum BREEAM standards, and BREEAM credits for innovation. The ratings for 2008, the latest update, include six levels of recognition, from unclassified (lower than 30 percent) to outstanding (85 percent and higher). A licensed organization performs a BREEAM assessment during the life cycle stages of a building. "Its scoring system is easily understood, and the method has had a positive influence on the design, construction, and management of buildings," claims Constructionbytes.com, a British building website.

BREEAM is not without its criticisms, however. One argument is that it weighs a building's space for parking and accommodations for bicycles over green structures and technologies. Another is that the rating system does not accurately measure a building's performance when it is occupied. "Total emissions are strongly influenced by tenant behaviour, from the type of fit-out, the number of people in the building and the hours the building is in use each day, to the amount of electrical equipment installed and the occupier's understanding of how to run the heating and cooling efficiently," says Mark Jansen, professional and legal editor of *Property Week*. "BREEAM makes assumptions about how the building will be used but inevitably, the reality is often very different," he maintains. In the following chapter, the authors investigate how eco-architecture is promoted by the architecture, building, and housing industries.

"The fact that an ecological approach does not exclude an aesthetic design is being proved by architects worldwide."

Stylish Design Will Encourage More People to Opt for Eco-Architecture

Inken Herzig

Inken Herzig is a journalist and an author based in Germany. In the following viewpoint, Herzig contends that architects incorporate strong aesthetic designs in sustainable building. Recent green projects around the world—from private residences to large-scale developments—showcase groundbreaking standards of energy efficiency, innovative use of green and recyclable materials, and architectural beauty, Herzig maintains. In fact, Herzig points out, architects suggest that sustainable building is required to improve the quality of life that the next generation already embraces.

As you read, consider the following questions:

1. How does the author describe the glass roof of the European Investment Bank?

2. What is the "triple-zero" standard, as described by Herzig?

Inken Herzig, "Combining Aesthetics with Efficiency," *Deutschland*, September 14, 2009. Reproduced by permission.

3. What does sustainable architecture mean, in the words of Matthias Sauerbruch?

The European Investment Bank in Luxembourg thrusts its way along Konrad-Adenauer-Ufer like a glistening ocean wave. These days a bank is hardly likely to win prizes for its services. But in this case it's the building that has been commended: as a successful example of sustainability. It's the first building on the continent of Europe to be awarded a British BREEAM [Building Research Establishment Environmental Assessment Method] certificate with a rating of "excellent". This eco-standards agency assesses the environmentally relevant aspects of a building from the planning stage through the construction period to its final use. The new building opened in June 2009 is overarched by a curving glass roof 170 metres long and 50 metres wide. The glass construction, which acts as both a winter garden and as protection against adverse weather conditions, is an aesthetic achievement for architect Christoph Ingenhoven and an engineering achievement for Werner Sobek. The duo had previously caused a stir worldwide with their spectacular "Lufthansa Aviation Center" in Frankfurt am Main, a building that uses only a third of the energy required by conventional buildings.

Modern Ecological Construction and Visual Effect

Christoph Ingenhoven is a specialist in the use of renewable energies and such resources as geothermal energy and rainwater. The German is one of the world's leading architects advocating sustainable and ecological architecture. He always designs his buildings according to international ecological standards on principle. Werner Sobek is an expert in state-of-the-art façade systems. He is Mies van der Rohe [Visiting] Professor at the Illinois Institute of Technology, Chicago, structural engineer and architect, and collaborates on large-scale projects worldwide with such international star architects as

Zaha Hadid, Norman Foster and Helmut Jahn. Yet one of his most pioneering buildings is his private home in Stuttgart. The elegant glass-and-steel cube demonstrates more than most buildings the kind of visual effect that modern ecological construction can generate. It is built according to the triple-zero standard, which Werner Sobek developed himself. This principle defines the requirements that a building must meet in order to be meet demands for sustainability. Werner Sobek's house needs no power (zero energy), emits no CO_2 (zero emissions), and will leave no waste behind when it is renovated or demolished (zero waste). This means that all the parts of the building can be fully recycled if, one day, no one wants to live in the building any more.

The German "Seal of Approval for Sustainable Building", awarded for the first time in January 2009, is also based on the triple-zero principle. It was developed by the German Sustainable Building Council (DGNB), whose president is Werner Sobek, together with the Federal Ministry of Transport, Building and Urban [Development]. The DGNB grants the new seal of approval to buildings that are eco-friendly, resource-saving and economically efficient, as well as comfortable and convenient for their users. In short, the DGNB certificate assesses all aspects of building according to the benchmark of sustainability. Demand for the German seal of approval is already booming; it is regarded as particularly reliable and of high quality by international comparison. Some 40 buildings are currently in the process of being certified. There are also initial signs of interest abroad in taking over the German certification method, or certifying buildings according to this standard

According to a survey by the Jones Lang LaSalle consultancy, more than 40 percent of Germany's companies intend to pay more attention to climate protection in the future when looking for offices or other premises. The percentage of eco-properties looks set to grow further, as such buildings are not only easier for property developers to market, they are also good for a company's image—generating a clear conscience in terms of environmental and climate protection. This is probably also one of the reasons why Deutsche Bank in Frankfurt is in the process of modernizing and renovating the façade of its shiny skyscrapers, turning them into "Green Towers".

Finance plays a role, too, of course. If you look at the costs of a building over its entire life cycle, only 20 percent stem from its construction; 80 percent are made up of subsequent running costs. Thus, in view of rising energy prices, aiming for optimum energy efficiency does more than make ecological sense. "The sustainability issue is a public matter, a res publica," says Werner Sobek. "We are making rapid progress because there is a lot of interest in the market," adds Christian Donath, CEO of the DGNB, and mentions the high level of demand for the new seal of approval. There are now twelve members of staff working at the Stuttgart office in the meantime, and some 600 organizations involved in homes and building are represented by the DGNB.

A Berlin-based group of architects, who came to the media's attention by collaborating with US actor Brad Pitt, works on the principle of beginning on a small scale what people discuss on a large scale. They are called "Graft Architects". They are currently planning a residential pavilion called the "0 Energy House" in Kuala Lumpur, Malaysia. Their aim is to offer discerning cosmopolitans top home comforts while consuming zero energy. The concept behind the almost 16,000-square-foot residential pavilion is that it integrates into the landscape as a dynamic structure. The living area is located at the core of the building; it provides a cool interior in the otherwise hot and humid climate. The entire building is made of renewable or recycled building materials.

Earth Friendly Does Not Equal Ugly

Banish the thoughts of earth shelter buildings and geodesic dome structures—bad ideas from the seventies (remember leisure suits were once "in" too). These days, earth friendly cannot be distinguished from the rest of the buildings in a neighborhood. Some of the most fabulously beautiful building materials available are green. For example, in green kitchens you'll find counters and backsplashes with gem-colored recycled glass tiles. Or look for natural, funky-colored Marmoleum or stained concrete floors. And don't forget less-toxic paints in all colors and natural, earth-type plaster applications for walls. All are gracing the pages of the most chic decorating magazines. Earth friendly can equal stylish, hip, and beautiful design.

Kim Carlson,
Green Your Work: Boost Your Bottom Line
While Reducing Your Carbon Footprint,
Avon, MA: Adams Business, 2009, p. 72.

Green Is No Accident

The young generation of architects in particular thinks "green" is no accident. "The green movement is not a temporary phenomenon. It's a necessity in order to improve the standard of living and quality of life for all people." Stefan Behnisch is convinced that "it makes sense to really make an effort on this issue." The architect is following in the footsteps of his father, Günter Behnisch, who became famous as the architect of the Munich Olympic site. Stefan Behnisch became interested in sustainability at an early age. "I grew up very much aware that our environment is an important and scarce resource. It was always a subject of conversation at home, too." Stefan Beh-

171

nisch has won several awards for his sustainable architecture projects. As early as 2002 the Stuttgart-based architect won the prize for environment-friendly building in Paris. The jury, chaired by Jean Nouvel, honoured him for two projects with a strong ecological orientation: the Institute [for] Forestry and Nature [Research] at Wageningen, Netherlands, and an office building designed for the Schleswig-Holstein social insurance institution (LVA) in Lübeck. Behnisch's latest works include the national Unilever headquarters in Hamburg's HafenCity, which was opened in 2009. The building for the 1200 employees meets the highest of environmental standards. It's the world's largest building with exclusively energy-efficient LED lighting. Stefan Behnisch also designed Germany's biggest new museum building: the spectacular "Ozeaneum" in Stralsund. Planned in the shape of four erratic boulders from the Ice Age, it tells the story of the oceans. Of course, sustainability was a priority in the planning of this building, too—but it's also architecturally exciting at the same time.

The fact that an ecological approach does not exclude an aesthetic design is being proved by architects worldwide, not only with museums, but with buildings that are veritable living sculptures. The Wall House designed by the German-Chilean architect duo FAR belong in this category. Marc Frohn and Mario Rojas Toledo were commissioned by a Chilean to design a detached residential house. With their Wall House the two young architects have developed a residential tent with walls that function like layers of clothing—using the multilayer or onion principle. Each layer has its own climatic, atmospheric and material characteristics which the residents experience like interacting clouds of sensory impressions and moods.

The American star architect Daniel Libeskind also has a sustainable approach to new projects. The man who designed the Jewish Museum in Berlin and drew up the master plan for Ground Zero [in New York City] can currently be seen in

Datteln, North Rhine-Westphalia, where a company called Rheinzink is erecting the "Libeskind Villa", a residential sculpture made of sustainable materials. The building also has a solar thermal plant in the roof, a geothermal power plant combined with a heat pump, and a rainwater system which helps to save precious drinking water. . . .

When Less Is More

For all their enthusiasm for ecological building, the first architects are now expressing criticism of the sustainability concept. "Everybody's talking about sustainability, and the word is often abused," says architect Matthias Sauerbruch, co-proprietor of the renowned firm of architects Sauerbruch Hutton in Berlin. Sauerbruch and his partner Louisa Hutton recently caused a stir when they built the Brandhorst Museum in Munich. Its façade, made of thousands of multicoloured ceramic rods, is reminiscent of an oversized abstract painting; inside the building its complex climate technology ensures ideal room temperatures. The building uses heat energy from the groundwater with the help of special heat-pump technology. The idea is to save about 50 percent of the thermal energy required for air conditioning compared to conventional systems. In the case of the Brandhorst Museum, the emphasis was not only on sustainable building criteria, but also on truthfulness. "For all our 'ecological correctness', in many cases the question is how sustainable is sustainability really," asks Matthias Sauerbruch. In his view, sustainable architecture means "when less is more. Buildings must be beautiful and well built, so that they can also be loved generations later."

Christoph Ingenhoven agrees. In addition to standards of energy efficiency and aesthetics, says the globally successful architect, there is a key requirement for sustainability in buildings: "We should concentrate on houses that are really needed. These days many people build for image reasons, and these buildings sometimes end up being pulled down again quite quickly. Green building issues should therefore be preceded by another question: Is it the right decision to erect the building at all?"

> *"The field of architecture is experiencing a design crisis, with clients . . . demanding that architects prioritize sustainability above all else—as if design itself were an obnoxious carbon-emitter."*

Green Building Blues: Is "Well-Designed Green Architecture" an Oxymoron?

Kriston Capps

Kriston Capps is an art critic based in Washington, DC. In the following viewpoint, he insists that eco-architecture lacks good design. Established architects are reluctant to work with new methods and materials, Capps claims, leaving sustainable projects to designers with fewer resources. Also, he suggests that both renowned and emerging firms have little experience with green building, resulting in a default "green" look of blocky glass structures. Linking the gap between eco-architecture and design will create desirable buildings and benefit the environment, the author declares, offering an opportunity for ambitious architects and builders to leave their mark.

Kriston Capps, "Green Building Blues: Is 'Well-Designed Green Architecture' an Oxymoron?," *American Prospect*, vol. 20, no. 2, March 2009, p. 35. Copyright © 2009 by The American Prospect, Inc. Reproduced by permission.

As you read, consider the following questions:

1. What were criticisms of the architectural designs for Vancouver's Olympic Village, according to the author?

2. Why do green architects and their clients see design as part of the problem, in the author's view?

3. What will happen when eco-architecture becomes an art form, in the author's opinion?

The Olympic Village in Vancouver will be a marvel of the 21st century once it is complete. Currently under construction for the 2010 Winter Olympics, the 1.4 million-square-foot, 16-building village will be outfitted with passive solar panels and green roofs and heated by a recycling apparatus that captures the heat emitted by sewage and redirects it back to the residences. Every building in the complex is designed to outlast its temporary use, and every building is made with its long-term carbon footprint in mind. For its efforts to leave no good turn unrecycled, the Olympic Village is hauling home enough Leadership in Energy and Environmental Design (LEED) gold and platinum medals to make an Olympic contender green with envy.

Yet for all its lauded environmental ingenuity, Vancouver's Olympic Village has limited ambitions when it comes to design innovation. Despite assurances from village project manager Hank Jasper that "you don't need sod walls and 30-foot trees on the roof to make it sustainable," the project's higher-ups rejected ambitious architectural designs for fear that they did not look green enough. Renowned postmodernist architect Robert A.M. Stern was originally chosen to lead the project, but his proposed design for the waterfront community center and other sites met with significant resistance from Vancouver. The city's senior urban designer, Scot Hein, declared to the *Vancouver Sun* that Stern's design was "not expressive of sustainability." Stern, the dean of architecture at

Yale University, was asked to leave the project, and a locally based architecture firm, Arthur Erickson Corporation, was hired in his place. But Erickson, too, was given neither the time nor the mandate to pursue lofty design goals. "There's not much play there," Erickson's partner Nick Milkovich told the *Globe and Mail* in January 2007.

With function prized above all else, the Olympic Village building designs have a default "green" look to them: blocky, all glass, covered in matted foliage. It looks as though the developers simply forgot to design the place.

The field of architecture is experiencing a design crisis, with clients ranging from private owners to cities demanding that architects prioritize sustainability above all else—as if design itself were an obnoxious carbon-emitter. This is partly because high designers and the so-called "starchitects," who fear that new methods and materials might not comport with long-established styles, are not taking the lead on sustainability issues, leaving green innovation to younger firms with fewer resources. Both well-known firms and up-and-comers lack experience in working with new, often expensive green materials, which has forced many designers to depend greatly on singular and design-restrictive tactics such as "passive design"—essentially, lots of space and windows—to achieve sustainability goals.

As a result, much green architecture reflects a quality that Ford's Edsel possessed: It looks like the future, but it doesn't look good.

One reason that emerging green architects and their clients have come to see design as part of the problem is that the most lauded design projects in recent history have made virtually no attempt at sustainability. "Look at the architecture of the last 15 years," says James Wines, a professor of architecture at Penn State University and the author of *Green Architecture*. "It's been more flamboyant and more wasteful than it's ever been before. To build any of these buildings by Frank

Gehry, it takes, what, 60 to 80 percent more metal and steel and construction than it would to enclose that space in a normal way. So you're talking about incredible waste. Mind-boggling waste."

As "green" becomes an increasingly valuable term to associate with any new building, architectural projects are claiming the label, whether or not they have paid attention to sustainability. "They say, 'Oh, the Getty Museum, Richard Meier, environmental,'" Wines says. But the Getty "carved out half a mountain and flew in all that travertine. Can you imagine the amount of trees and gallons of fossil fuels it took to fly in all that marble? It's insane."

So-called "greenwashing" has contributed to both the hype and the shoddy design standards associated with green building. Though the advent of formal certification processes like LEED has cut back instances of out-and-out fraud, greenwashing has no doubt devalued the currency of the term "green" and often obscures more complex conceptual problems. Developers in Florida, for example, have taken to recycling shipping containers to create affordable homes, only to plop them into carbon-inefficient suburban communities without retrofitting them in a way that is energy efficient. Shuhei Endo's Slowtecture M arena in Japan is similarly problematic. Its natural lighting and trendy sod exterior may make up for the energy-inefficient steel in the skeleton, but insulation can't offset the carbon emissions of sports fans driving to its isolated location outside the Kobe suburbs.

Architects are divided on what constitutes a truly sustainable building. Transporting efficient materials long distances to build green is a problem in the eyes of architects like Wines, who thinks about materials in the way that Alice Waters does about food. "It's better to build with what you have in Pittsburgh"—that is, steel—"than to import the wood from Seattle," Wines says. This approach emphasizes a regional, integrated standard for sustainability that might not adhere to the materials-based focus of LEED certification—a ribbon that green architects know they need to pin to their projects. Confounding the matter is the nature of new materials and strategies, which call for study and experimentation beyond the means of many firms, no matter how enthusiastic they may be. Established architects—those with the most resources—often prefer to let their brand drive their work, green materials be damned.

Stefan Behnisch is a German architect whose firm, Behnisch, Behnisch & Partner, is best known in the United States for the Cambridge, Massachusetts, headquarters of the biotech firm Genzyme—a dazzling, LEED-platinum-certified building with 12 light-filled stories of open atrium. He is critical of other big-name architects who resist going green. "Established firms like to do stuff the way they always have done it. They are not flexible. They are corporate quality plans, and they don't allow innovation. It took them very long to catch on."

But those name-brand firms still exclusively focused on formalist innovation look increasingly isolated on their fake islands in Dubai. The field's high stylists prefer materials like titanium—an environmental abomination. Further, they often use quite immodest amounts of these materials to enclose a space. The architectural style that persists among the very top performers is Baroque and epic at a time when the rest of the field—the rest of the world—is turning to questions of content (in other words, a building's purpose). Those questions are largely about sustainability, an issue on which architectural leaders refuse to lead. "Architecture has so many bad habits that it can't change easily," Wines says. "I think most architects are terribly threatened by the green movement. Because God forbid they have to change the style. What if any one of us leading stylists had to change their style simply because you can't build with that material anymore?"

In recent projects, Behnisch has managed to deviate from the orthogonal unit that drives green architecture, allowing for curved, organic features and other ornamental elements. This is no mean feat: Thermal glass, which keeps in heat more efficiently, does not curve readily. Behnisch says that information about new materials represents the biggest lag on design progress within the field. "In the early '90s, when we first started out, we had to do a lot of research," he says. Today, many of Behnisch's clients—including the Catholic Church, which he describes as the most demanding green client in the world—arrive at the table well versed in new materials and building methods. One of Behnisch's frequent haunts is a meta-architectural research firm in Stuttgart that focuses exclusively on studying new materials.

Wines, for one, has faith in architects' ability to adapt. "There's a lot of materials that are very, very good from an ecological perspective," he says. "You learn to invent with those."

Behnisch thinks it is inevitable that green architecture will grow out of its awkward stage. "[Green building] will inform the architectural development," he says. "It's still content-driven. We have a new topic—a new and very interesting topic—to inform the architecture. Once we marshal the subject to its own formalistic approach, the design will move architecture further, but it is still developing."

What might finally bridge the gap between design and environmentalism is the realization that good design is also good for the environment. "If it isn't art, it's not sustainable, because who's going to keep ugly buildings around?" Wines asks. Sustainability could be considered the broader architectural framework into which green architecture fits. As Behnisch told *Metropolis* magazine in December, "I never saw a discrepancy between design and sustainability. I always felt that sustainability could drive architectural form."

When sustainable architecture coalesces into something more like art, it will likely be more in keeping with a world teetering on the brink of economic and environmental collapse than with the architectural modes that preceded it. Further, the sustainable school may well dial back the lessons of globalization, preferring instead to adopt a new regionalism and to find virtue in the frugal rather than in the profligate, expressing these preferences through design. Wines sees the very real potential for a fundamental reimagining of what architecture means, the sort of revolutionary revision that took place when Le Corbusier introduced the International Style. "The idea of a building as a piece of sculpture is 100 years old now," Wines says. "It's been done over and over and over. It's not very progressive as a premise."

These questions are finding an audience beyond the world of architecture, as President Barack Obama has signaled a moment for action unrivaled since Franklin Roosevelt's Works Progress Administration.

"What I've seen thus far and have been excited about is the recognition of the role that the built environment plays in issues such as climate change, issues such as energy security," says Tom Hicks, vice president of international policy and programs for the U.S. Green Building Council. He tickets the built environment (primarily buildings, but all man-made surroundings) for 39 percent of the nation's carbon emissions. "There's a huge opportunity for us to turn that back."

While the starchitect class has all but entrenched itself in an opulent style out of sync with the rather serious issues facing humans and our environment, emerging architects are taking solace in green architecture. Determining just what sustainability in architecture means is bound to yield the same innovation in design that the Industrial Revolution did for the modernist style.

From the academy to the builder, green architecture—and the long-term promise of sustainability—is an opportunity for workers to profit and for designers to make a name. In the long term, it dares to marry the built and natural environments, the standoff at the heart of the architectural dialogue between man and nature. And perhaps sooner rather than later, it will produce some buildings we can grow to love.

| "Many more people believe that LEED is an important third-party certification for green buildings and that most owners genuinely wish to do the right thing within the constraints of their values and budgets."

The LEED Rating System Helps Create Greener Buildings

Helen Kessler

Created by the US Green Building Council in 1998, Leadership in Energy and Environmental Design (LEED) is a point-rating system that recognizes four levels of sustainability. In the following viewpoint, Helen Kessler claims that LEED certification promotes green building practices in commercial and residential development. The methods in which it measures criteria and standards constantly evolve, she contends, which allows for updates as sustainable concepts are defined. Furthermore, Kessler continues, LEED has changed the way firms approach the design process, increasing interaction and input among architects, design teams, and stakeholders. The author is a principal of HJKessler Associates, a green design and consulting firm in Chicago, Illinois, and a LEED-certified professional.

Helen Kessler, "Using LEED the Right Way," *Building Operating Management*, October 2007. Copyright © TradePress, 2007. Reproduced by permission.

As you read, consider the following questions:

1. As stated by Kessler, what are builders' motivations behind LEED certification?

2. According to Kessler, what is the problem with awarding LEED points for bike racks?

3. How did a change in LEED's minimum level of energy efficiency affect design teams, according to Kessler?

The sustainable design movement has gained immense popularity in commercial and institutional real estate nationwide. According to the U.S. Green Building Council (USGBC), the green building market is expected to exceed $12 billion in 2007, with approximately 3 percent of new commercial developments in the United States pursuing LEED [Leadership in Energy and Environmental Design] certification.

Clearly, commercial properties are being influenced by sustainable design principles. But sometimes projects may not be as holistically green as they could be. That's because motivations for incorporating green strategies vary. Motivations may include one, some or all of the following: reduce long-term operating costs, attract tenants, provide a more comfortable and productive environment for employees, be a good environmental steward, reduce the time required to get a building permit (e.g., Chicago's Green Permit program), or obtain the public relations benefits that LEED certification may bring.

Some detractors claim that LEED is nothing more than a marketing ploy. However, many more people believe that LEED is an important third-party certification for green buildings and that most owners genuinely wish to do the right thing within the constraints of their values and budgets. Facility executives should consider the apparent gaps between marketing, social and environmental issues and smart business.

All too often, developers, owners, designers and facility executives only go after the low-hanging fruit, earning upon a project's completion the right to say that a property is LEED certified without having made a significant commitment to resource efficiency or good indoor environmental quality much beyond business as usual.

One particular recurring complaint about LEED always seems to revolve around bike racks. In most major cities, there are bike racks everywhere around town. Most would agree that bicycle riding is a good environmental strategy because it relies on human energy as opposed to petroleum. Simply providing a safe place to lock bikes and a place to shower may encourage people to ride their bikes to work or exercise during the middle of the day, and LEED provides a credit for incorporating those strategies into a building.

However, it is important to consider the particular project. If it's a project in a rural location, then the bike racks are superfluous and not really a green strategy at all. Yet the same number of points can be earned for including them as can be earned by using a cool roof or other more expensive energy-related technologies.

Evolution Is Coming

LEED is evolving; it is a grocery list of measures that meet current criteria and standards, with a nutrition label that demonstrates a project's level of greenness. As with any list, it can be updated and modified at any time. USGBC has been gathering input from a wide variety of stakeholders and adding strategies that will receive Innovation in Design points. Think of this model as the next evolution of a particular software suite. It's a means of updating LEED and thinking about sustainable design concepts without issuing a whole new version of LEED.

For instance, a relatively new concept much discussed recently is the zero-energy building. There are many definitions of zero energy, only some of which actually translate into a very efficient building. Given current technology and know-how, a building that uses about 50 percent less energy than a traditional building should be very possible if the owner, facility executive and design team take an integrated approach and use creative thinking to reduce the size of heating and cooling systems. However, simply going for zero energy by purchasing renewable energy credits may not be the smartest policy, as money could be better spent to improve building efficiency.

The building team should ask important questions: How can the most resources be saved? What resources should be saved? In the process of saving resources, are the goals for the building being met?

It is important to consider how to maximize the efficiency of systems so the overall construction and long-term operating costs are minimized.

A New Way to Draw the Lines

Having a gold or silver certification is not just about hanging a pretty plaque on a lobby wall or adding a section to a marketing pamphlet. For some project teams, using LEED means thinking about design in a new way. Traditionally, design has been linear—the architect makes the initial design decisions based on input from the owner and the rest of the team follows the architect's lead. Input is provided by both owner and developer, but the central hub is with the architect first and then the rest of the design team.

Remember the "quality circle" approach? Members of teams offered input on ways to improve the quality of the product or process. That is similar to what LEED can accomplish if a team follows an integrated approach.

A good place to start on the LEED process is a goal-setting workshop (often called an eco-charrette or sustainable design charrette) at a project's inception. On projects that start with such a meeting, it's evident that the project takes shape much

A Green Paradigm Shift

LEED [Leadership in Energy and Environmental Design] itself was not intended to be used as a standard on every building, but rather to highlight the leaders within the industry, encouraging others to jump on board with green building, and thereby create a paradigm shift. Instead of having to look specifically for materials with recycled content, for example, or for "green" alternatives to cabinetry to incorporate into a design, such a paradigm shift would mean that all available materials would be based on recycled content and there would no longer be an option for non-green cabinetry. In sum, the market itself—and all of the available options within it—would be inherently green.

Traci Rose Rider,
Understanding Green Building Guidelines:
For Students and Young Professionals,
New York: W.W. Norton & Company, 2009, p. 14.

quicker and the design team and owner come to a clear agreement about the goals for the project.

The eco-charrette sets the direction for the project and provides a framework for going forward. When goals are set early and all of the project stakeholders are included in the process—including owner, facility executive, building occupants and maintenance personnel—the project team has a much easier time making value judgments when it comes time to make tough budget decisions.

Commercial and institutional property owners can set their projects apart by incorporating design concepts that touch as many internal and external environmental conditions as possible. Employee well-being—things like comfort levels, good indoor air quality, high-quality lighting and daylight, and the like—are often melded with corporate initiatives such as corporate growth and values and financial flexibility to uncover new ways to improve a property.

Incorporating external environmental considerations, like natural resource use, recyclability and reductions in pollution is important and has a broader social component. Connection to community and government channels are two rapidly growing issues in which properties are being asked to add value, as property is just as much a part of an economic landscape as any money spent within it.

If facility executives consider green design principles before a site is selected (as opposed to later in the design process, or, even less optimally, when construction begins), it is much easier to have that site approved by all parties and, thus, achieve high-performance goals that meet LEED certification.

Equally important is fully understanding site conditions and what can be achieved. For example, during a charrette for a gut rehab of an existing, nearly windowless building, the fact that employees wanted good daylight and indoor air quality to optimize their productivity was discussed. By identifying sustainable design goals such as these, the design team could focus on the systems that would have the most impact on the facility occupants. In this case, significant daylight was added to the building through the use of both clerestories and new windows. The goals outlined during the charrette became a powerful incentive for the building owner not to cut costs in those areas.

It goes without saying that change takes time, and green building in general and LEED specifically are still in their infancy. LEED is already forcing design teams to work more closely together and think about systems and ideas that they might not have previously thought about. This is crucial to getting beyond thinking about LEED as a checklist of credits that can be achieved one by one.

USGBC recently made an important change to LEED—requiring a minimum level of energy efficiency above the energy standard it had previously used—which now forces design teams to think more carefully about energy use and hopefully to come up with better systems. There's still work to be done in this area, but things seem to be moving in the right direction.

As facility executives, architects, engineers and contractors continue to work together and learn more about building green, it's possible to advocate for higher standards of sustainable design that provide lasting environmental solutions and help create a better tomorrow.

> "One of the reasons you'll find very few
> critics out there is that lots of folks
> make money on LEED."

The LEED Rating System
Is Not Effective

Anya Kamenetz

In the following viewpoint, Anya Kamenetz questions the integrity of Leadership in Energy and Environmental Design (LEED), the voluntary rating system established by the US Green Building Council, in fostering green architecture. The Architecture 2030 initiative, which is adopted by many firms, has much more stringent energy-saving requirements than LEED, she points out. Moreover, the categories of the rating system are not regionally adjusted or even weighted, Kamenetz persists, meaning that the same points are awarded for building features that are not equally sustainable. LEED, however, is a leading green standard and valuable marketing tool and has very few opponents. Kamenetz is a senior writer and columnist for Fast Company *and was nominated for the Pulitzer Prize for feature writing in 2005.*

As you read, consider the following questions:

1. What is an obstacle to assessing the effectiveness of LEED, in Kamenetz's view?

2. What is the business case for LEED certification beyond saving money on energy, as told by the author?

3. In the author's opinion, what was the initial goal of LEED, and how should it be adjusted now?

When this magazine [*Fast Company*] moved to 7 World Trade Center this past spring [in 2006], we were pleased to be settling into the first New York office tower to score a "gold" for environmental sustainability from the United States Green Building Council, or USGBC. Buildings account for 71% of America's electricity use and 38% of all greenhouse gas emissions, according to the Department of Energy. Anything that cuts those numbers—as USGBC-certified buildings do, by an average of 25% to 30%—is surely a plus.

But what does the plaque on the front of a $700 million glass tower really mean? Asking that question exposes some serious cracks in the world's biggest green building brand name—Leadership in Energy and Environmental Design, or LEED—as well as a very human tendency to reach for easy solutions to difficult problems.

As alarm over the environment intensifies, LEED has been in the right place at the right time. Two federal agencies, 22 states, and 75 localities from Seattle to Boston have instituted policies to require or encourage LEED; in New York, the new rules are expected to affect $12 billion in new construction in the next few years. A host of major New York projects, including new luxury condos in Battery Park City, a 2-million-square-foot skyscraper on Bryant Park in midtown, and the rest of the buildings around the World Trade Center site, have all sought the council's stamp of approval.

But critics say that the LEED standard falls short of what's possible in terms of saving energy. While a 25% to 30% improvement in energy use over conventional buildings sounds impressive, it pales compared with, say, the 50% target adopted by the dozens of firms that have signed on to the Architecture

2030 initiative. Assessing LEED is further complicated by the business growth of the Green Building Council. Awarding gold—and silver and platinum—certification has been a gold mine for the nonprofit organization. Once a small operation with seven paid employees, it now fields a 116-member staff and earns 95% of its $50 million annual budget.

Which raises another question: Could the council's financial success be standing in the way of cutting-edge green building standards?

Driving the Market in a Green Direction

The Green Building Council started 14 years back with an unlikely alliance between a real estate developer, David Gottfried, and a senior scientist for the Natural Resources Defense Council, Rob Watson. "The great majority of environmental organizations had invested in keeping companies on the other side of a fence," says Richard Fedrizzi, the current CEO of the council. "David [Gottfried] thought that we could do things differently. If we could invite business to the table, we could develop standards relative to building performance, buy in at the very top, and be able to transform the marketplace toward sustainable buildings."

The result, introduced in 2000, was LEED. The LEED rating system is simple in concept. Architects and engineers shoot for points in six categories: siting, water use, energy, materials, indoor air quality, and "innovation in design." Once a building is complete, a representative from the Green Building Council reviews the documentation—plans, engineers' calculations—and awards points out of a possible 69: certified (at least 26 points for new construction), silver, gold, or platinum (at least 52 points).

Watson says the point system was specifically constructed to entice builders and drive the market in a green direction. "One definable action equals one point," he says. Bike racks, one point; recycling room, one point. "We threw a few gimmes in there so people could get into the low 20s . . . and say, 'We can do this.'"

And it worked. Power-suited developers and hard hats have signed on. More than 6,500 projects have registered for LEED certification since 2000, and new categories such as commercial interiors and existing buildings have been added to the original LEED for new construction. Forty-two thousand people have paid $250 to $350 and passed exams to become "LEED-accredited professionals."

The council's revenue has been growing at 30% or better a year, with close to 20% coming from certification. Getting the LEED plaque is not cheap. In February, the mayor of Park City, Utah, told a building-industry publication, "On the Park City Ice Arena [$4.8 million project cost], we built it according to LEED criteria, but then we realized that [certification] was going to cost $27,500. So we ordered three small wind turbines instead that will power the arena's Zamboni."

Much of this growth is credited to Fedrizzi, a former marketing executive for an air-conditioning company who became CEO in 2004. "We realized we were getting the messaging wrong, leading with the environmental story," he says. "We had to lead with the business case."

A Whole New Commercial Ecosystem

The business case isn't just that green building saves money on energy. It's that LEED certification sells buildings to high-end clients and governments, gets architects and builders sparkling free publicity, and creates a hook for selling new products, materials, and systems to builders. It's a whole new commercial ecosystem. "Here in DC," says architect Russell Perry, who's active in the Green Building Council, "for a speculative developer to go out and advertise their property as being Class A [the highest quality commercial building], they've got to have a LEED rating. The brokers need that as part of their pitch. People who would have been ambivalent about that as a moral issue are finding that it's a commercial necessity." Perry also cites the mushrooming of markets for products and services such as less toxic paints.

Fedrizzi is now talking to holders of multibillion-dollar real estate portfolios, such as Cushman & Wakefield and Transwestern, about the possibility of trading carbon credits from green buildings.

Even skeptics recognize the council's achievement. "There's nothing else out there. LEED is what's for dinner," says Auden Schendler, the director of environmental affairs at Aspen Skiing Co. and the author, with Randy Udall, of a much-discussed 2005 article in Grist, the online environmental [website], titled "LEED Is Broken: Let's Fix It." "Plus, it's a good idea. Previously, nobody knew what a green building was."

But, Schendler adds, "one of the reasons you'll find very few critics out there is that lots of folks make money on LEED. And it is a bit of a cabal—it's like criticizing the pope in Rome. People don't want to alienate themselves from this great emerging movement."

The Limitations of LEED

The limitations of LEED proceed from its design. The categories aren't weighted, meaning that a bike rack, to use an oft-cited example, can get you the same point as buying 50% of your energy from renewable sources. And there are no regional adjustments; saving water earns a point in Seattle just as it does in Tucson. What's more, says Schendler, "until recently, you could certify a building to LEED with no energy measures." Now beating a widely accepted international baseline (ASHRAE [American Society of Heating, Refrigerating, and Air-Conditioning Engineers]/IESNA [Illuminating Engineering Society of North America]) by 14% is required. But is that enough? "All 10 points [in the LEED energy category] should be mandatory," Schendler asserts. That would mean

Grades of Greenness

LEED [Leadership in Energy and Environmental Design] ratings are not given by any popularly used metrics (such as BTUs [British thermal units] of energy consumed per square foot per year) but by names of metals including *silver, gold* and *platinum* for the levels of certification. Bronze was the original rating for the lowest level but was replaced with the term "*certified.*" Uses of metal names to make an association with Olympic sports prizes rather than some more scientific way of rating makes measuring and comparing difficult. Jerry Yudelson, in his book *The Green Building Revolution*, says "Since Americans are competitive and obsessed with keeping score, the LEED system is particularly well suited to our culture."

As stated above, LEED has multiple ratings which are essentially "grades of greenness." One might compare LEED ratings to school grading with *platinum* being an A, *gold* a B, *silver* a C, and *certified* a D. This nomenclature is somewhat confusing since the term certification, which includes all buildings in the four grades, is also the title of the lowest grade (*certified*). Thus certified is used in two ways that can be confusing, e.g., the LEED building was certified *gold* or the LEED building was certified as "*certified.*"

Pat Murphy,
"Special Report: Part 1: LEEDing from Behind:
The Rise and Fall of Green Building,"
New Solutions, *May–June 2009.*

beating the ASHRAE baseline by 42%—which, he says, "is achievable and frankly isn't even enough to solve the climate problem."

The temptation for developers and builders is point mongering—picking one action from column A, another from column B. "I think people have the idea that sustainability is just a collection of exciting ideas that you can peel and stick onto your building," says David White, a climate engineer with the German firm Transsolar. "Unfortunately, the exuberant creative stuff—the expensive buzzwords such as 'geothermal,' 'photovoltaic,' 'double facade,' and 'absorption chiller'—only make sense when the basic requirements, such as a well-insulated, airtight facade with good solar control, are satisfied."

Jerry Yudelson, who has written five books on LEED and marketing green buildings, highlights the peel-and-stick method in his forthcoming book *Marketing Green Building Services: Strategies for Success*. He calls solar panels and green roofs "two of the most important emerging green technologies." Yet most engineers say that solar panels have limited applications on large buildings, and reflective roofs can save as much energy as "green" ones covered with plants. But Yudelson writes, "Nothing beats publicity like having your project, with its green roof, PV [photovoltaic, or solar power] system, and LEED gold plaque highlighted as a lead story on the 6 o'clock or 10 o'clock network news station in your city. You'll get on camera; dozens, possibly hundreds of clients, prospective employees, and others in your industry will see it, almost guaranteed."

New York architect Chris Benedict—whose residential buildings use only 15% as much energy for heat and hot water as the typical New York apartment building—says, "I've spent hours explaining my systems-based approach to a newspaper reporter, and at the end, the photographer asked me, 'Do you have a solar panel or something I could photograph?'" With her design partner, Henry Gifford, a former boiler mechanic, Benedict delves into the infrastructure of buildings, incorporating basic factors such as heavy-duty insulation, radiant heating and cooling, room-by-room temperature controls, and thicker glass.

Benedict, who works outside the LEED structure, says that environmental constraints free her creativity, citing a building in the Bronx where dramatically deep sills shade the south-facing windows. Certain clichés of modern architecture, like the glass curtain walls of One Bryant Park, the future headquarters of USGBC board member Bank of America, are another story. "It's pretty frustrating that there's going to be a LEED platinum-rated glass building," Benedict says. "It's going to use obscene amounts of energy. At times, it will need to be heated and air-conditioned at the same time."

Jordan Barowitz, director of external affairs at the Durst Organization, the developers of One Bryant Park, counters, "You could make a building that's very energy efficient by not having any windows in it and having only one elevator, but this is not a building that people are going to want to work in."

So what should define a green building? It's not necessarily shiny or pretty, and it starts from the minute the site is chosen. LEED began with the goal of getting attention for energy-efficient building. Now that it is dominant in the marketplace, it could be adjusted to better reflect—and exploit—its new-found power.

Rob Watson, the so-called father of LEED, seems to agree. "Over the last 10 years, the gravity of the global environmental situation has become more obvious," says Watson, reached in China, where he's consulting on green buildings for the government and private developers. "And so I think, if anything, we need to redouble our efforts, and not only go for greater market share but increased stringency at the same time."

"Instead, the [homeowners associations] are holding steady on [green building] restrictions and seem to be looking at everything on a case-by-case basis."

Some Homeowners Associations Will Take Eco-Friendly Practices into Consideration

T.Q. Jones

In the following viewpoint, T.Q. Jones writes that some home-owner associations (HOAs), which manage residential subdivi-sions and communities, individually evaluate green building practices on residents' properties. As energy conservation and cli-mate change become a wider concern for homeowners, HOAs' policies on prominent sustainable devices and structures, such as rooftop solar panels and water-saving gardens, make room for technological advances, Jones states. However, he explains, asso-ciations vary in their restrictions, and what may go uncontested in one neighborhood may cause problems in another. Jones is a writer for the Oak Hill Gazette *in Austin, Texas.*

As you read, consider the following questions:

1. In Larry Lane's view, why does his architectural committee judge green home practices by each case?

2. According to Jones, why is the Zarsky house able to have its unique eco-friendly features?

3. What are HOAs' current views of rooftop solar panels, as stated by Jones?

As energy costs escalate on every front, Americans are finally beginning to think about alternatives, either in fuel generation to replace what we are losing or lifestyle changes to reduce the amount we need. It's possible both of those might force changes in our neighborhoods, with battles being joined over installing solar panels or wind generators, or replacing your once-lush lawn with a cactus garden.

But in talking to several of the homeowners associations (HOAs) in and around Oak Hill (Texas), the *Gazette* found no such neighborhood strife so far in Oak Hill. Instead, the HOAs are holding steady on restrictions and seem to be looking at everything on a case-by-case basis. One reason, according to Larry Lane, who is on the architectural committee at New Villages of Western Oaks, is the fact that technology is moving so fast.

"We could go in and rewrite our standards," he said, "but they might be outmoded in a year. It's better to look at every case as it comes up. We'd rather not have solar panels on the front of a house, but we'll look at it." One might think the restrictions in older neighborhoods would be less rigorous than those in the newer and more expensive subdivisions, but both Shady Hollow and Circle C had solar panels on the roofs of some homes. And Steve Urban, the new president of the Circle C homeowners group, echoed Lane's comments about technology being ahead of guidelines.

"We have 20 or 25 homes with solar panels and we're working with our homeowners, but setting guidelines would be trying to hit a moving target." Both Lane and Urban agreed that some of the technological changes would probably also lead to changes in the appearance of something like solar panels and allow greater use of them.

In fact, New Villages at Western Oaks actually installed solar panels, that are nearly unnoticeable, to power the entrance lights of the neighborhood—unfortunately creating an attraction for vandals and thieves that has meant putting the idea on hold, though the panel structures are still in place.

One goal of "green" building is sustainability, which might be defined simply as not using up resources faster than the earth is able to replace them, but most people probably agree that we aren't doing a very good job at it. Instead, we keep burning fossil fuels, which harms the earth on at least two fronts; by using up a resource in fossil fuel that is being depleted and can't be replaced, while polluting the atmosphere as it does so.

A Reputation for Tolerance

Austin has a reputation as a tolerant (if occasionally weird) city, and John Rosshirt of Stanberry and Associates, a "green builder" who also has experience managing a homeowners association, expects homeowners and homeowners associations to adapt.

"Homeowners associations exist to do what their homeowners want, and to protect property values," he says, "and the homeowners may well ask for changes in the restrictions of the association if necessary." He notes there are stories about enforcement gone overboard (such as an association foreclosing on a home because the homeowner wouldn't keep his grass cut), but those stories are rare. (Those we talked to were more concerned someone might get the bright idea to put his solar array in the front yard, thus also avoiding the need to mow the lawn.)

Kathy Zarsky, a graduate architect with 12 years of working in construction management who now works as a sustainability consultant, notes that everything isn't equal about putting up solar panels or wind generators, either.

"With solar panels, it's important that they be oriented correctly and at the right angle. If your roof faces the wrong way, you'll have a less efficient system. Wind turbines generally work best if they are about 100 feet up, so that can cause problems."

We actually first went to talk to Kathy and Jon, her husband, because they have a concrete house with a "vegetative garden roof." That is, they have a large section of roof that is planted with plants similar to, if not identical to, what grows on the ground around the house.

The rooftop garden is part of a plan that will eventually include capturing and holding rainwater, among other things, to help make their house (which is very well designed) more energy efficient and less dependent on outside sources. As Kathy notes, concrete is very strong, but has a terrible energy-efficiency value, so the roof garden also helps lower energy costs.

Unfortunately in some ways, they are far enough away to be out of the Austin Energy power grid and on Pedernales Electric Cooperative, which means no incentives from the power company for "building green." Under the garden is a large, one-piece membrane like a big shallow bathtub that lets water through, but slowly. The soil is the same as the soil around the house, and is nutrient poor.

"The [Lady Bird Johnson] Wildflower Center helped us a lot," Kathy says. "We gave them the soil information and they gave us suggestions as to what plants would do best. The city has been monitoring our runoff and testing the water. Preliminary results indicate the water coming off the roof is the same as the runoff from undeveloped land."

Solar Access Laws

In the later days of ancient Rome, a combination of enlightenment about the tremendous power of the sun and energy constraints resulting from overharvesting of nearby firewood led to the enactment of solar access laws. Many homes throughout the Roman Empire were heated by the *heliocaminus*, or "solar furnace"—a south-facing room that stayed warm in the winter. As the population increased and the built environment expanded, these rooms became shaded, leading to a ruling in the second century A.D. that a home's access to sunlight could not be violated by one's neighbors. This ruling was eventually incorporated into the Justinian Code of law.

Likewise, English common law—upon which both United States and Canadian law is based—provided for solar access through the law of ancient lights. Essentially, this says that if a building has had access to the sun for twenty years, then no structure may be erected to shade it. It is also likely that this arose because of the incorporation of solar heating and lighting into English homes, and the resource limits of depleted firewood supplies. As of this writing, there are no known cases of the law of ancient lights being enforced in North America.

We believe we are at the cusp of a similar dynamic, where fossil energy's limits (both its availability and its intolerable pollution), combined with an awareness of solar energy's amazing potential, is leading to the adoption of laws that not only prohibit ordinances that stymie solar installations, but go one step further in guaranteeing a property's access to the sun.

Stephen Hren and Rebekha Hren,
A Solar Buyer's Guide for the Home and Office: Navigating
the Maze of Solar Options, Incentives, and Installers,
White River Junction, VT: Chelsea Green Publishing, 2010, p. 23.

Which was another point made by both Lane and Urban. Xeriscaping doesn't mean letting the lawn go until it takes over the house, so even if the guidelines allow the use of native plants that don't use a lot of water, there may still be restrictions on just what you can do with your "natural" lawn.

Because their kind of rooftop garden is currently a rarity, Kathy says a couple of hundred people have come to look at it, but she cautions that what works for her might not work somewhere else.

"You have to decide what you want from a vegetative garden roof and talk to people like the Natural Gardener and the Wildflower Center, the folks with the expertise." So how is the roof garden doing? Kathy spot watered it to help get it started, it looks great (naturally with hardy plants), and she hasn't watered it now since October.

A Wild Variety of Architecture

There are other considerations, of course. Though well designed and efficient, Kathy and Jon's home wouldn't necessarily fit in the average neighborhood, which is why they built it on 15 or so acres and not visible from the road. It's likely only the neighbors who have been invited over have any idea what the design of the house is. It's also likely a house designed the way this one is would also fit very well in an area such as Westlake, which has a wide variety of neighborhoods with a wild variety of architecture.

Lane noted his group had handled one request for a metal roof which was declined, but that doesn't necessarily mean all metal roofs would be turned down. As Urban noted, in the case of Circle C, some requests might hinge on which "neighborhood" in Circle C was involved, because Circle C isn't one homogenous group of homes, but a group of several neighborhoods with different "looks." What "fits" in one might not look the same in another.

That doesn't mean the neighbors might not go bananas if you strung a clothesline in the backyard instead of buying another dryer, but as Rosshirt pointed out, it sometimes depends on whether anyone is bothered by it. A restriction that didn't exist (because who was worried about solar panels on roofs in 1961?) can be added at the request of the homeowners, just as one can be eliminated by the same process.

One of the newer homeowners groups has a simple restriction regarding solar power that reads, "Solar equipment. All usage of solar equipment must be approved in writing by the architectural committee." While that pretty well covers the bases, it doesn't ban solar panels. As Rosshirt points out, the restrictions usually exist to help protect property values, and are there because the homeowners want them there.

A complication is that with existing technology it isn't efficient to send electricity over long distances, so the most efficient way to have solar or wind power at your home is to have solar or wind power at your home, rather than sending it through wires from any distance. Which in turn means you will have to do something the neighbors might notice, put up solar panels or stick a wind generator on top of the house.

Perhaps expecting not many homeowners associations would allow solar panels, legislation has been introduced that would bar the associations from banning them. But even those people from the homeowners associations who didn't want to be quoted were in agreement that it wouldn't be a matter of banning solar panels, just of making sure they passed muster with the architectural committee.

And, as Lane, Urban and Rosshirt all pointed out, technology keeps getting better. In fact, Rosshirt was one of several people who suggested that in ten or fifteen years, solar panels would be more efficient and look just like ordinary roof tiles.

| *"Most associations have not caught up to the green innovations."*

Obtaining Homeowners Associations' Approval of Eco-Friendly Practices Is Difficult

J. Roger Wood

Homeowners associations (HOAs) are groups created by residential builders or developers to regulate subdivisions and enforce restrictions. In the following viewpoint, J. Roger Wood maintains that green practices—rooftop solar panels, compost piles, even clotheslines—attract opposition from HOAs and neighbors for flouting aesthetic community standards. HOAs that allow them are the exception, and existing property laws and contractual agreements are often too complex for state legislation to force green practices, he asserts. Planning for sustainability at the development stage, Wood insists, is the best way to promote it to HOAs and communities. The author is a partner at Carpenter Hazlewood Delgado & Wood, a law firm based in Arizona and New Mexico, and represents HOAs and condominiums.

J. Roger Wood, "HOAs Going Green with a Bit of Kicking and Screaming," *Construction Law Musings*, June 18, 2010. Copyright © 2010 Construction Law Musings-Richmond, VA. Reproduced by permission.

As you read, consider the following questions:

1. How does the author describe ownership and common areas in condominiums?

2. According to Wood, why doesn't enacting laws help homeowners associations deal with greening issues?

3. What are the benefits of going green at the development stage, as claimed by Wood?

A t our law firm, we are experts on homeowners association and condominium association law. We have clients in Arizona and New Mexico. From the 10 unit condominium project to the 12,000 lot master-planned community, we deal with green issues when HOA [homeowners association] boards and neighbors square off on solar panels, clotheslines and compost piles, among others. From our vantage point, everyone likes the idea of green until it means too much glare from the shiny panels on the neighbor's house. The clothesline isn't a problem until you have to stare out your kitchen window at your neighbor's drawers all day. Most board and association members I meet want state legislators to make good environmental protection laws, so long as those protections don't cause a stink (literally) in the neighbor's backyard.

That's when boards start calling us, the HOA lawyers. Some boards fight the changes and can't imagine why the law would require an approval of those "ugly" solar panels on the neighbor's roof. Other boards of directors vote to acquiesce and do attempt some reasonable aesthetic modification to placate green owners and complaining owners alike. But in my recent pit stops on the road to HOA sustainability, I've come across a few observations that might help us all with getting to green.

The Green Temperature in Most Communities Is Sub-Zero to Cold with a Few Hot Spots Scattered Around the Country

Whether you believe [former vice president and climate change activist] Al Gore or not, and no matter the cost savings or the benefits to our environment of "going green," many board members have been reluctant to bend community aesthetic standards for one homeowner's request for a green modification. Oh the hours of board meetings we have attended to quibble over inches of visible solar collectors on the rear face of a neighbor's rooftop. Boards are reluctant to swallow the perceived bitter pill of green initiatives as a whole and even more reluctant to make changes to their own governing documents to accommodate environmental trends. Most associations have not caught up to the green innovations.

There are a few exceptions to the rule and the awareness of the clash between green and most HOA CC&Rs [covenants, conditions, and restrictions] and architectural guidelines is growing. Just last month [May 2010], the green versus HOA issue hit the big time. *The Colbert Report* ran a short, snarky piece about an Oregon woman battling her HOA over a clothesline. Both hilarity and thoughtful discussion ensued.

A few HOAs are the exception, where grassroots movements have sprouted up and homeowners are working together to communicate with neighbors about greener HOA policies. The website Sustainablecreekside.org is an example of one such effort where some Oregon neighbors have created an Internet site to help communicate, organize and promote green initiates in their own community. However these few bright spots and spirited discussions continue to be overshadowed by the NIMBY [not in my backyard] crowd.

Enter the state legislatures.

State Legislatures Are Trying to Force a Robust and Square Peg of Green Ideas into the Very Round Hole of Existing Law and HOA Documents

I am aware of many state lawmakers passing (or in even more cases, attempting to pass) legislation to force green regulation on community associations. Here in Arizona, there were several bills introduced in our legislature this year that would have allowed homeowners to install or operate various energy-saving devices. These proposed bills would have allowed owners to ignore contractual deed restrictions and install and operate an energy-saving device free from any HOA scrutiny and regulation. Our Arizona legislature proposed bills about clotheslines, rainwater harvesting systems, and awnings for shade. Due to our state's budget woes, the bills did not get out of the legislature and to the governor's desk. However, several passionate legislators (and their lobbyists) have vowed to introduce similar green bills again next year.

One of the troubling issues about forcing green into some of the same existing communities with existing standards and restrictions is that often state legislatures show little consideration for contractual CC&Rs or for other existing state laws that regulate much about HOAs and condos. In many situations, the new laws would make implementing green impracticable and in some cases legally impossible.

For example, this year the Arizona House of Representatives introduced HB 2778. This bill would have amended Arizona's condominium statutes and planned community statutes. The bill would have allowed homeowners to ignore existing HOA/condo deed restrictions (CC&Rs) and install "rainwater harvesting systems that are intended to act as a water-saving device." The bill went on to give associations some rights about aesthetics and placement, but the HOAs could not have prohibited these water-saving devices.

It doesn't sound too terrible or too complicated. Water conservation is good, right?

But there is a serious square peg/round hole problem here. The bill would have allowed an association to decide how the water collection device looks, but the bill would have done nothing to contemplate the legal realities of a condominium. Many condominium owners only own the space bound by the four walls of the unit. The rest of the property is usually defined as some type of a common element, co-owned in undivided equal interests by all of the owners in the project. Oftentimes, condominium restrictions require the condo association to maintain those common elements, which are to be paid for by the assessments of all. The language of this bill would have contemplated a situation whereby one neighbor's 100-gallon water tank could be stored on a second-story, common element balcony. The homeowner may have the right to occupy and use the balcony, but who maintains the system when the association is obligated to maintain the balcony itself? Are the balconies designed to withstand an additional 800 pounds of water weight? Who pays premiums to insure the system? Does legislating green really have to risk the health and safety of the downstairs unit owner?

The Most Logical and Least Painful Greening Is Happening at the Development Stage

Thoughtful legislation may be one way to go green, but perhaps those laws are best made to help developers who create and build the communities. Starting from scratch with the development and creating of a green neighborhood avoids the square peg/round hole problem altogether. Proposing and passing new laws and municipal building codes that impose greener practices on residential builders and developers may be the best way for HOAs and condos to dive into the green movement. This is not only about construction standards, but it should be about requiring developers to draft documents that encourage green rather than restricting those kinds of modifications.

Sweeping and radical changes to the 30-year-old condominium project will likely only grow and cultivate litigation, and in the end, that's only good for me, the HOA lawyer. Influencing green development, construction and HOA formation will inevitably lead to marketing the kinds of homes consumers want to buy and the kind of sustainable communities where home buyers want to live.

Using Virginia as an example, its legislature recently reacted to some studies by smart urban planning types who have written to warn of the ill effects of cul-de-sacs on our communities and the health of our planet. These experts posit that cul-de-sacs challenge public transit plans, result in more driving, discourage walking, are more expensive for municipalities to maintain and can even make us fatter. Virginia legislators made a new law to limit the construction of cul-de-sacs in new developments by allowing municipalities to suspend maintenance of cul-de-sac roadways. The commonwealth's new law requires green from the get-go, saves money and fuel expenses at the local level and does not impose new restrictions on any already established cul-de-sac communities. Green is already part of these communities before anyone buys the first lot.

Green residential construction projects are popping up all over the country. The market for green housing and the attention on these kinds of projects is gaining popularity. Perhaps the economy has slowed interest, but a quick Google search yields an abundance of information about who is building green residential projects and the location of some of the greenest neighborhoods around the country.

A recent *Wall Street Journal* article chronicles the story of one such green development. Owners at Riverhouse in New York City were marketed and sold green condominium units.

The posh condo development is at the river's edge on Manhattan's lower west side and the developer/builder fetched a pretty penny for the promise of a sustainable life and the highest of green building standards. The lure of green was so strong that when condo owners began to have problems with their units and the building as a whole, they filed a lawsuit alleging construct defects and alleging that the builder did not construct the community up to the proper and promised LEED [Leadership in Energy and Environmental Design] standards. If you want to know, "not green enough" comes with a $4.2 million claim. If you build it (green), they will come (for green), and if you don't build it green enough, it will cost you.

Riverhouse may be an extreme example, but incorporating green from the beginning may be the best and simplest way to turn the tide and change some minds on the residential side. Grassroots green efforts inside of communities build hostility and make lawyers richer. New legislation, without some very thoughtful statutory language and a complete understanding of the HOA/Condo structure (they never seem to ask us), will only frustrate association leaders and legislators alike. Once again, the lawyers benefit.

The path to green of least resistance starts at the beginning, a raw plot of land and a dreamer with an idea. Builders and developers have never had problems making that dream a reality and then marketing the next, best new home idea. When builders market and sell house-proud and community from a row of well-staged model homes, why not sell sustainability right alongside all of the upgraded appliances and marble countertops? It's not that I don't relish a good compost pile fight, but the mudslinging about green deserves a better starting point.

Periodical and Internet Sources Bibliography

The following articles have been selected to supplement the diverse views presented in this chapter.

Theresa Agovino	"Gold Standard for Green Buildings Under Fire," *Crain's New York Business*, January 2, 2011.
Daniel Brook	"It's Way Too Easy Being Green," *Slate*, December 26, 2007. www.slate.com.
Taryn Holowka	"LEED v3," *ED+C*, July 2009.
Ben Ikenson	"Is LEED the Gold Standard in Green?," *Miller-McCune*, June 13, 2011. www.miller-mccune.com.
Sophie Lambert	"LEEDing the Way for Neighborhood Development," *Sustainable Facility*, July 2009.
Tracy Loew	"Green Practices Conflict with Homeowners Associations," *USA Today*, May 13, 2010.
Catherine Salliant	"Solar Panels Causing Some Storms," *Los Angeles Times*, November 30, 2009.
Ginetta Vedrickas	"Modular Housing: Green, Stylish and Yours for Just £30,000," *Independent*, March 17, 2010.
Norman Weinstein	"Green Architecture's New Goal: Stylish Sustainability," *Christian Science Monitor*, July 11, 2008.
Kylie Wroblaski and Janelle Penny	"Innovating or Interfering?," *Buildings*, April 2011.
Greg Zimmerman	"Developers Are Embracing LEED, and Tenants Are Responding," *Building Operating Management*, December 2008.

For Further Discussion

Chapter 1

1. Teresa Burney warns that the use of sustainable materials and technologies increases the chances of litigation. In your opinion, does she provide a persuasive case? Use examples from the text to support your response.

2. Shannon D. Sentman contends that sick building syndrome (SBS) is a major concern and promotes Leadership in Energy and Environmental Design (LEED) to address the condition. However, John Wargo maintains that LEED standards for energy efficiency worsen indoor air quality by trapping harmful substances and gases inside buildings. In your view, which author presents the most urgent issue? Why or why not?

Chapter 2

1. Jane Powell declares that the most sustainable building practice is to extend the life of a building rather than construct a green one. Do you agree or disagree with Powell? Why or why not?

2. Jason F. McLennan insists that square footage determines a house's sustainability, proposing the enforcement of maximum home sizes per occupant. In your opinion, does the size of the house that Blair Kamin describes, which is too large by McLennan's estimates, negate its eco-friendly features and technologies? Cite examples from the viewpoints to explain your answer.

3. Robert Bruegmann contends that the concept of sprawl lumps together real and trivial problems facing cities and communities. In your view, does Pamela Blais do this in her viewpoint against sprawl? Why or why not?

Chapter 3

1. Jay B. Freedman advises that building practices and products may be greenwashed. In your opinion, is it possible that Peter W. Bardaglio, Jonathan Hiskes, or Karen Sandrick engage in greenwashing in their viewpoints? Use examples from the texts to support your response.

2. Jason F. McLennan, in his interview with Jonathan Hiskes, believes that eco-architecture standards must be raised and no new sites for buildings should be allowed. Do you agree or disagree with this view? Why or why not?

Chapter 4

1. Kriston Capps suggests that green architecture has become uniform and bland in design. In your view, do the projects and structures Inken Herzig describes disprove Capp's claim? Cite examples from the viewpoints to explain your answer.

2. Helen Kessler states that LEED has promoted green building practices in both commercial and residential development. However, Anya Kamenetz says that LEED has become a powerful marketing tool. In your opinion, which author makes the most persuasive argument? Why or why not?

3. J. Roger Wood insists that homeowners associations (HOAs) have not caught up with the movement toward green building practices. Do you agree or disagree with the author? Use examples from the texts to support your response.

Organizations to Contact

The editors have compiled the following list of organizations concerned with the issues debated in this book. The descriptions are derived from materials provided by the organizations. All have publications or information available for interested readers. The list was compiled on the date of publication of the present volume; the information provided here may change. Be aware that many organizations take several weeks or longer to respond to inquiries, so allow as much time as possible.

Alliance to Save Energy
1850 M Street NW, Suite 600, Washington, DC   20036
(202) 857-0666
website: http://ase.org

Founded in 1977, the Alliance to Save Energy is a nonprofit coalition of business, government, environmental, and consumer leaders that supports energy efficiency as a cost-effective energy resource and advocates energy-efficiency policies. To carry out its mission, the alliance undertakes research, educational programs, and policy advocacy; designs and implements energy-efficiency projects; promotes technology development and deployment; and builds public-private partnerships in the United States and other countries. Its website features a number of reports, position statements, and policy summaries.

American Society of Heating, Refrigerating, and Air Conditioning Engineers (ASHRAE)
1791 Tullie Circle NE, Atlanta, GA   30329
(800) 527-4723 • fax: (404) 321-5478
e-mail: ashrae@ashrae.org
website: www.ashrae.org

Established in 1894, the American Society of Heating, Refrigerating, and Air Conditioning Engineers (ASHRAE) is an international organization that works to advance heating, ventilation, air conditioning, and refrigeration to serve humanity and promote a sustainable world through research, standards writing, publishing, and continuing education. In addition to a national conference, ASHRAE regularly publishes position papers, *ASHRAE Journal*, *ASHRAE Insights*, and several newsletters.

Energy Star Program

1200 Pennsylvania Avenue NW, Washington, DC   20460
(888) 782-7937 (STAR YES)
website: www.energystar.gov

In 1992 the US Environmental Protection Agency (EPA) introduced Energy Star as a voluntary labeling program designed to identify and promote energy-efficient products to reduce greenhouse gas emissions. In 1996 EPA partnered with the US Department of Energy, and the Energy Star label is now on major appliances, office equipment, lighting, home electronics, and more and covers new homes and commercial and industrial buildings. In addition to annual reports and regular podcasts, the Energy Star website offers a number of publications, including energy-saving advisory reports, guidelines for new homes, and checklists for home improvements.

Environmental News Network (ENN)

(732) 968-2314
website: www.enn.com

Since 1993 the Environmental News Network (ENN) has been educating the world about environmental issues. Its website offers environmental news, daily feature stories, audio, video, blogs, and more in an effort to provide unbiased information about current environmental debates. Along with its *ENN Dial Newsletter*, areas of interest covered on its website include green building, environmental policy, climate, energy, pollution, ecosystems, and wildlife.

Environmental Protection Agency (EPA)

Ariel Rios Building, Washington, DC   20460
(202) 272-0167
website: www.epa.gov

Since 1970 the Environmental Protection Agency (EPA) has been working for cleaner, healthier water, land, and air to protect human health and the environment. EPA works to develop and enforce regulations that implement environmental laws enacted by Congress. EPA is responsible for researching and setting national standards for a variety of environmental programs and delegates to states and has responsibility for issuing permits and for monitoring and enforcing compliance. In addition to maintaining a database of environmental-related hotlines and clearinghouses, EPA offers a number of online publications, including "The Inside Story: A Guide to Indoor Air Quality" and "Healthy Buildings, Healthy People: A Vision for the 21st Century."

Healthy Building Network (HBN)
2001 S Street NW, Suite 570, Washington, DC   20009
(202) 741-5717 • fax: (202) 898-1612
e-mail: info@healthybuilding.net
website: www.healthybuilding.net

The Healthy Building Network (HBN) is a national network of green building professionals, environmental and health activists, socially responsible investment advocates, and others who are interested in promoting healthier building materials as a means of improving public health and preserving the global environment. Specifically, HBN focuses on the elimination of polyvinyl chloride (PVC) plastics, plywood and chipboards, formaldehyde, and wood treated with copper chromium arsenate in new and refurbished construction. In addition to an e-newsletter, HBN offers fact sheets and overviews on building materials.

Smart Growth America (SGA)
1707 L Street NW, Suite 1050, Washington, DC   20036
(202) 207-3355
website: http://smartgrowthamerica.org

Smart Growth America (SGA) is a coalition of national, state, and local organizations working to improve the ways cities and towns are planned. The coalition includes many national organizations advocating on behalf of historic preservation, the environment, farmland and open-space preservation, and neighborhood revitalization. The SGA website offers a number of resources, including publications such as "Building for the 21st Century: American Support for Sustainable Communities" and "Policy Analysis: Source Water Protection."

Sustainable Buildings Industry Council (SBIC)
1112 Sixteenth Street NW, Suite 240, Washington, DC   20036
(202) 628-7400 • fax: (202) 393-5043
website: www.sbicouncil.org

Established in 1980, the Sustainable Buildings Industry Council (SBIC) is an association of building associations committed to high-performance design and construction in conjunction with the fields of architecture, engineering, building systems and materials, product manufacturing, energy analysis, and "whole building" design. In addition to providing online tools and guides for building industry professionals, SBIC also publishes a monthly newsletter.

United Nations Division for Sustainable
Development (UNDSD)
Two United Nations Plaza, Room DC2-2220
New York, NY   10017
(212) 963-8102 • fax: (212) 963-4260
website: www.un.org/esa/dsd/

The United Nations Division for Sustainable Development (UNDSD) provides leadership and is an authoritative source of expertise within the United Nations system on sustainable development. The UNDSD maintains a database of world statistics on sustainability and a collection of news reports on current sustainable activities in world nations. In addition to position statements and FAQ sheets, the UNDSD website offers a number of other publications.

US Green Building Council (USGBC)
2101 L Street NW, Suite 500, Washington, DC   20037
website: www.usgbc.org

The US Green Building Council (USGBC) is a nonprofit organization composed of more than twelve thousand organizations from across the building industry working to advance structures that are environmentally responsible, profitable, and healthy places to live and work. USGBC's major effort is Leadership in Energy and Environmental Design (LEED), a voluntary, consensus-based national rating system for developing high-performance, sustainable buildings. USGBC offers online courses and other educational materials, including an online LEED Project directory and case studies e-books.

World Green Building Council (WGBC)
c/o Build Toronto, Toronto, ON   M5H 3T4
 Canada
website: www.worldgbc.org

The World Green Building Council (WGBC) is a union of national councils whose mission is to accelerate the transformation of the global property industry toward sustainability. Since 1999 the WGBC has served as the main voice for the green building councils that it represents and has supported the development and use of green building rating systems, such as LEED and Energy Star. In addition to worldwide sustainable building case studies and regional newsletters, its website offers a number of publications and reports, including "Tackling Global Climate Change" and "Six Continents, One Mission."

Bibliography of Books

Will Anderson — *Homes for a Changing Climate: Adapting Our Homes and Communities to Cope with the Climate of the 21st Century.* London, UK: Green Books, 2010.

Peter Bardaglio and Andrea Putman — *Boldly Sustainable: Hope and Opportunity for Higher Education in the Age of Climate Change.* Washington, DC: National Association of College and University Business Officers, 2009.

Williams T. Bogart — *Don't Call It Sprawl: Metropolitan Structure in the 21st Century.* New York: Cambridge University Press, 2006.

Robert Bruegmann — *Sprawl: A Compact History.* Chicago, IL: University of Chicago Press, 2005.

Neil B. Chambers — *Urban Green: Architecture for the Future.* New York: Palgrave Macmillan, 2011.

Dan Chiras — *Power from the Sun: A Practical Guide to Solar Electricity.* Gabriola Island, BC: New Society Publishers, 2009.

Wendell Cox — *War on the Dream: How Anti-Sprawl Policy Threatens the Quality of Life.* Lincoln, NE: iUniverse, 2006.

Ann V. Edminster — *Energy Free: Homes for a Small Planet.* San Rafael, CA: Green Building Press, 2009.

Marcus Fairs   *Green Design: Creative Sustainable Designs for the Twenty-First Century.* Berkeley, CA: North Atlantic Books, 2009.

Edward L. Glaeser   *Triumph of the City: How Our Greatest Invention Makes Us Richer, Smarter, Greener, Healthier, and Happier.* New York: Penguin Press, 2011.

Dolores Hayden   *Building Suburbia: Green Fields and Urban Growth, 1820–2000.* New York: Pantheon Books, 2003.

David Johnston   *Green from the Ground Up: A*
and Scott Gibson   *Builder's Guide: Sustainable, Healthy, and Energy-Efficient Home Construction.* Newton, CT: Taunton Press, 2008.

Sabrina Leone   *Eco Structures: Forms of Sustainable*
and Leone Spita   *Architecture.* New York: White Star Publishers, 2010.

Howard Liddell   *Eco-Minimalism: The Antidote to Eco-Bling.* London, UK: RIBA Publishing, 2008.

Jeffrey C. May   *My Office Is Killing Me!: The Sick Building Survival Guide.* Baltimore, MD: Johns Hopkins University Press, 2006.

Martin Melaver   *The Green Building Bottom Line: The*
and Phyllis   *Real Cost of Sustainable Building.*
Mueller, eds.   New York: McGraw-Hill, 2009.

Martin O'Donnell *Solar Energy for the Home: The Facts About Solar Panels.* Charleston, SC: CreateSpace, 2010.

Randal O'Toole *The Best-Laid Plans: How Government Planning Harms Your Quality of Life, Your Pocketbook, and Your Future.* Washington, DC: Cato Institute, 2007.

David Owen *Green Metropolis: Why Living Smaller, Living Closer, and Driving Less Are the Keys to Sustainability.* New York: Riverhead Press, 2009.

Linda Reeder *Guide to Green Building Rating Systems.* Hoboken, NJ: John Wiley & Sons, 2010.

Phyllis Richardson *Nano House: Innovations for Small Dwellings.* New York: Thames & Hudson, 2011.

Traci Rose Rider *Understanding Green Building Guidelines: For Students and Young Professionals.* New York: W.W. Norton & Company, 2009.

Shay Salomon *Little House on a Small Planet: Simple Homes, Cozy Retreats, and Energy Efficient Possibilities.* Guilford, CT: Lyons Press, 2010.

Sarah Susanka and Kira Obolensky *The Not So Big House: A Blueprint for the Way We Really Live.* Newtown, CT: Taunton Press, 2009.

Galina Tachieva *Sprawl Repair Manual.* Washington, DC: Island Press, 2010.

Index